Also by Steven Stoll

The Fruits of Natural Advantage:
Making the Industrial Countryside in California

Larding the Lean Earth:
Soil and Society in Nineteenth-Century America

U.S. Environmentalism Since 1945:
A Brief History with Documents

The Great Delusion

The Great Delusion

A Mad Inventor, Death in the Tropics,

and the Utopian Origins of Economic Growth

Steven Stoll

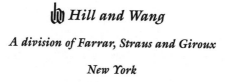

Hill and Wang

A division of Farrar, Straus and Giroux

New York

Hill and Wang
A division of Farrar, Straus and Giroux
18 West 18th Street, New York 10011

Distributed in Canada by Douglas & McIntyre Ltd.
Printed in the United States of America
First edition, 2008

Parts of Chapter 4 originally appeared in Harper's Magazine.

Library of Congress Cataloging-in-Publication Data
Stoll, Steven.
The great delusion : a mad inventor, death in the tropics, and the utopian origins
of economic growth / Steven Stoll.— 1st ed.
    p.   cm.
Includes bibliographical references and index.
ISBN-13: 978-0-8090-9506-3 (hardcover : alk. paper)
ISBN-10: 0-8090-9506-8 (hardcover : alk. paper)
    1. Conservation of natural resources—United States—History.   2. Utopias—
United States—History.   3. United States—Economic conditions.   4. Etzler, J. A.
(John Adolphus)   I. Title.

S930 .S86 2008
338.973—dc22

                                                                2008018113

Designed by Jonathan D. Lippincott

www.fsgbooks.com

1   3   5   7   9   10   8   6   4   2

For Howard Lamar

The premises from which we begin are not arbitrary ones, not dogmas, but real premises . . . They are the real individuals, their activity and the material conditions under which they live. —Karl Marx, *The German Ideology* (1846)

Howsoever we may succeed in making ourselves more space within the limits set by the constitution of things, we know that there must be limits.

—John Stuart Mill, *Principles of Political Economy* (1849)

Contents

∾∾∾

Illustrations

ॐॐॐ

The Great Delusion

Double the Economy!

ᠵᠧᠵᠧᠵᠧ

I know the exact moment when I began to think about economic growth. It happened in 1996 while I was watching the televised vice presidential debate between Al Gore and Jack Kemp. Responding to a question by journalist Jim Lehrer about whether it would be possible to "balance the budget without reforming drastically the entitlement programs, including Social Security and Medicare," Kemp lit up in a corona of Republican energy: *"We should double the rate of growth and double the size of the American economy. This means more jobs, more wealth, more income and more capital, particularly for our nation's poor and those left behind!"*[1] I don't recall anything else about the debate. It struck me then that doubling the economy meant doubling the rate of making everything—the disposable coffee cups, cans of air deodorizer, copper pipe, jumbo jets, canned tuna. If Kemp had drawn out his meaning and spoken longer, he might have said this: "If the United States would only double the size of its economy, using the unlimited resources of the earth to do so, the created wealth would elevate everyone to a higher standard of living, eliminating the need for entitlement programs." In this view, poverty requires no domestic policy, no redistribution of wealth; rather, we eliminate it by increasing the transfer of matter and energy from environments into the economy. Kemp not only believed that the earth could sustain a doubling of American patterns, he saw a doubling as the fulfillment of a social vision. *Growth* will spread the joys of consumption to every blighted street from East St. Louis to Johannesburg. *Growth* will spark a transition to modern living and governance in the poor nations of the world. *Growth* will unify humanity by dissolving class distinctions—all without sacrifice.

There are certain places where the scope and scale of economic growth come into view, where I stop, as though gazing over the Grand Canyon, and just wonder. One of those canyons is Costco. It begins with shopping carts broad enough to seat two children side by side. The carts had better be big. They need to haul one-gallon jars of mayonnaise, 117-ounce cans of baked beans, 340-ounce jugs of liquid detergent, and 70-ounce boxes of breakfast cereal. The coolers advertised for summer picnics hold 266 cans. Giant warehouse stores, shelved to the ceiling with goods from all the waters and forests of the world, make no excuses for consumption. But though Costco sells its goods in large packages, there is no item here that cannot be found at a corner grocery. Then why don't I lighten up and buy a pallet of mango salsa? Because thundering all around me is the scope and scale of American economic growth. Here it is possible to witness the enormous throughput of the economy—its capacity to mobilize resources and energy and turn out waste. One store manager, on the floor for fourteen years, told me that he has seen eight pallets of paper towels move out the door in a single day—that's forty packages to a pallet, twelve rolls to a package, or 3,840 rolls. I can hear the sound of chain saws laying off as falling trees cut the air somewhere high in the Cascades. The question that comes to my mind whenever I catch a glimpse of aggregate consumption is always the same: How can it last?

It is a discomforting question. Growth is tangled up with the way we think about nature and society. Beginning in the early nineteenth century, it took over almost the entire meaning of progress. But why write a book critical of something that safeguards the health and security of so many? Who would argue against more production, consumption, and trade? These are universally wanted because they offer the possibility of greater security from want. Growth has made possible lower rates of child mortality, widespread opportunities for education, and the private-sector technology that powers our ever-greater productivity. Any critic who does not consider the astounding benefits of growth ignores the common experience of billions of people. I do not question its accomplishments, but the more I learn about the assumptions underlying it, the more I am sure that it exists in a bubble. Disturbing as it sounds, growth on the scale known to industrial societies over the last two centuries is a historically exceptional condition that carries with it all sorts of doubtful ideas about the relationship between society and nature. We want to believe that one day, everyone on earth will know a 2.5 percent annual increase in gross domestic product (GDP), that the human family will live in sufficiency and comfort. People who sense dependable subsistence do certain hopeful things—they marry and have children, increase their consumption, and thus cause an outward shift in the entire economy, amplifying commerce, employment, and demand—in a positive feedback loop promising that most fundamental of human desires: a more durable existence. My concern is that this loop exists in its own imaginary world.

In this book I am not interested in the incomes of Americans, or in worker productivity, or in the American growth curve, but in the quest itself. When did people begin to think that any society could escalate in wealth and consumption without limit, that a nation could enter a period of constant, ever-rising expansion? At stake is an entire conception of humanity and the environment, mediated through the relationships and institutions we call the economy. Growth seems so institutionalized, so sure. Word of it on the nightly news comes in measures that distance it from the gritty stuff without which there is no economy. But no rise in the stock market or the residential construction index can be detached from the availability of the metals and fibers fabricated into everything. There exists an unsettling disconnect between our hoped-for lives and the failure of Economy to communicate with Ecology. The disconnect is simple. Modern economies expand, but the ecosystems that provide for them do not. They *change*—pine gives way to oak, coyotes arrive in New England, invasive grasses take over a marsh—but they do not *increase*. Anything that dies becomes a buffet for the reabsorption of its matter/energy by other organisms. At some point early in the nineteenth century, the commercial economies of Britain and the United States began to step up the rate at which they turned natural capital into consumable products. A steam-engine pace of production shattered the ancient solar ceiling, driving the production system at a pace beyond the capacity of ecosystems to regenerate or restore.[2] Political economists of the nineteenth century did not see that happening. For them, the greater pace of production became an expression of nature itself.

I weave this problem through a biography. I first had the idea to write this book after reading *The Paradise Within the Reach of All Men*, written by a German engineer who immigrated to the United States in 1831. John Adolphus Etzler pursued universal abundance in order to eliminate class conflict and poverty. His scientific thinking, combined with his belief that he could deliver endless wealth to billions of people within the observable laws of the universe, indicated stunning changes taking place during the late eighteenth and nineteenth centuries and pointed toward an emerging conception of material progress. The thinkers featured in these pages sketched out many of the assumptions that continue to describe our environmental relationships. Like Etzler, we expect more of everything, if only in the passive reassurance that the leading economic indicators gained in the last quarter and that the jobless rate fell. We tacitly assume—simply by the way we live—that the transfer of matter from environments into the economy is not bounded by any condition of those environments and that energy for powering our cars, dehumidifiers, leaf blowers, and iPods will always exist. We think of growth as progress. Separating these long-connected ideas is like peeling apart leaves of ancient parchment stored so long in clay jars that they have petrified into one mass. But doing the separating reveals that they are, in fact, distinct, that there can be one without the other: progress does not depend on economic growth, and economic growth does not always lead to human progress. In order to confront epoch-making problems, that distinction must be made and its history traced.

Etzler saw himself (as Kemp did) standing at the beginning of an unprecedented expansion that would sweep away misery and social inequality. Without in any way condemning the goal of improving the human condition, it is time to rethink the particular conception of progress that such thinking represents. Now that the Intergovernmental Panel on Climate Change has unequivocally implicated economic activity as an uncontrolled experiment in changing the chemistry of the earth's atmosphere, the initial justification for accelerated material progress seems relevant. As it turns out, Etzler's dreams and schemes existed squarely within the materialist thought of the early nineteenth century, and his basic assumptions can be traced to the beginnings of economics as we know it. And while Kemp the conservative and Etzler the Hegelian socialist might seem to belong at two extremes along the political spectrum, their differences are not nearly as important as their similarities.

CHAPTER ONE

A Philosophical Machine

ᠵᡄᠵᡄᠵᡄ

They rolled it out of the shed before daybreak, heaving it with men and horses to where it stood the morning long, in the ordinary dampness of the field. The directors of the Tropical Emigration Society arranged with a local member of the gentry for the use of the pasture near Oxford, England, renaming it Satellite Field for the occasion. Gunshots and church bells rang out before noon, and people gathered with bottles and blankets to watch what promised to be more than just another rake-and-reaper show—rather, a world to come, a kind of revelation. Its inventor designed it to do anything on the ground: plow, pulverize and sift soil, level a field, sow grain, pull weeds, cultivate between plants, mow, harvest, hammer, saw, cut down trees, pull out stumps, notch rocks, excavate and elevate, dig ditches and canals, form terraces, operate in water or mud, dig mines, and generate its own power. It was a Swiss Army knife on wheels, a cross between a plow and the Batmobile. The inventor devised other marvelous things that he promised would capture the abundant and available forces of the earth: a Naval Automaton powered by ocean waves, as well as a floating island covered with fertile soil, supporting houses, halls, and windmills. But nothing surpassed the Satellite in its transformative power, in the vastness of its meaning. The country people would witness a conduit of energy that would liberate them from authority and custom, a tool toward the creation of a completely cultivated and populous earth, the prime mover behind a community that would be exemplary for all communities—a philosophical machine.

We know it only from its blueprint. It consisted of an iron frame nearly forty feet long and eighteen feet wide—about the dimensions of a shipping container. Two long, rotating beams mounted on top extended its length to fifty-seven feet. Massive wheels carried it at the front end, smaller ones behind. Its forward motion turned a roller that could be fitted with teeth for planting or spades for digging. Add a hopper for seeding; attach blades for harrowing; connect ropes and wheels for pulling anything; snap on brushes, shovels, boards, saws, and hammers as needed. A truck for collecting ran alongside. No horses, no engine. It looked more like the Mars rover Leonardo da Vinci might have invented than an agricultural implement.

Its energy came from a square-shaped reservoir surrounded by twelve windmills. The windmills lifted water into the reservoir, which filled to the level of a spillway, from where the water fell 100 feet onto a wheel. The rotating wheel pulled a series of wire lines thousands of feet long, each wrapped around a wooden pivot. The turning pivot transferred energy from the wire lines to ropes connected to the Satellite. To understand the shape it created, draw a line ending in a point; then draw a radius off of the point at any angle, like the hour hand of a clock; then draw the circle implied by the radius. But the Satellite didn't go round and round in the same circle. The ropes could be shortened or lengthened to change the machine's distance from the pivot,

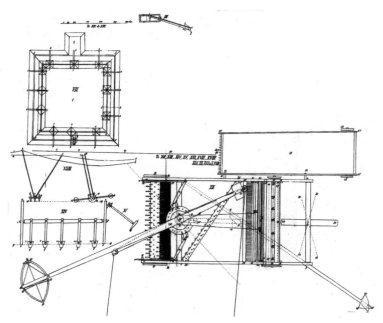

The Satellite. Etzler's design for a machine that would generate infinite wealth by concentrating infinite power on infinite resources can be difficult to decipher. This top view of the machine shows its rotating beams and a roller fitted with spikes. A truck for collection runs alongside. The same illustration features the reservoir and windmills. Note the smaller version of the Satellite, placed to establish scale. (Courtesy Yale University Library)

resulting in a spiral pattern as the contraption worked its circle inward or outward, sowing or cutting trees or harvesting wheat or digging ditches. Think of the circular fields created by pivot irrigation on the Great Plains. Each is about 2,600 feet in diameter, or half a mile. On paper, the Satellite had a maximum radius of 1,000 feet, enclosing about 70 acres as it wound inward, tracing a furrow like a snail shell. Gawky in its details, the Satellite makes a different impression from high above its trajectory, seemingly as elegant and certain in its orbit as the moon.

Every form of production changes space in characteristic ways. A landscape formed by peasants cutting wheat with scythes looks different in its scale and patterns from one formed by a steam-driven reaper. As a spatial system, Etzler's model had a single overarching purpose—replication. The Satellite would subject vast regions to mechanical discipline, driven by its determining machine. An observer at cruising altitude would take in branches splitting off from every 4,000-foot central line, creating a hexagon of eighteen orbits, together enclosing about 1,400 acres (including the spaces between the circles). The inventor called this pattern a *circuit*. Fifty-five circuits formed a *dominion* of nearly 80,000 acres, twelve miles wide. The history of humankind told a

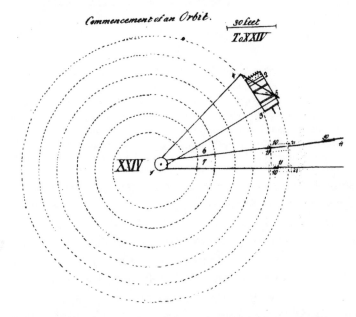

Orbit, Circuit, and Dominion. The Satellite created its own land system, one that could be infinitely extended in a geometrical pattern. (Courtesy Yale University Library)

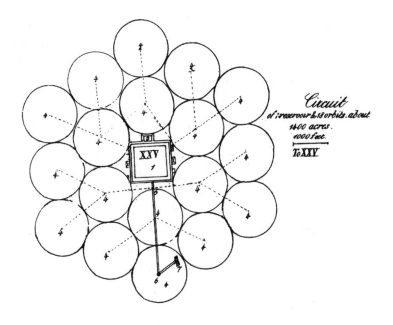

Circuit
of 1 reservoir & 18 orbits. about
1400 acres.
1000 feet.

To XXV

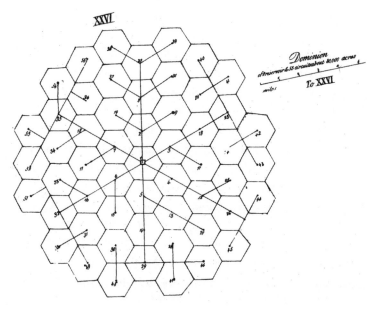

XXVI

Dominion
of 1 reservoir & 55 circuit about 80,000 acres

To XXVI

miles

story of drudgery and scarcity, with people flailing helplessly to open the great chest of abundance standing in plain sight. With the Satellite as their key, the starving multitudes had it in their power to overturn the structure of society without violence, causing a social revolution that no industrialist or aristocrat could ever stop. The inventor promised that those "who are poor and of the labouring classes," who earn but "a poor pittance for sustaining life," would soon delight in 20,000-acre gardens "cultivated by three or four men, with but one dollar of capital (once forever) per acre," and would then "live like gentlemen and ladies."[1]

The benevolent colonizer behind the promises, the trickster scientist who somehow shrouded the most detailed blueprints in fog and night, was John Adolphus Etzler. He was not in England or even in the temperate latitudes at the time of the demonstration. His last communication came from Venezuela, reporting on his negotiations with the minister of foreign affairs for land on which the Satellite would operate. By 1845, Etzler provided the intellectual leadership for a thriving organization of believers who anticipated machinery to usher in their freedom from crippling factory work and horrifying poverty. The South American venture also involved Etzler's partner, publisher, and interpreter, Conrad Stollmeyer, who remained in England to work out the details of the construction and testing of the Satellite. The mechanic in charge in England, however, found it difficult, whether by a lack of skill or materials, to follow every detail of Etzler's design, so he built a smaller machine—four feet wide and twenty feet long—and improvised in other ways as well. Awaiting the reservoir and windmills that would plug it in to the earth's perpetual motion, the Satellite moved under the force of a steam carriage set in the middle of the pasture, the two connected by a six-hundred-foot rope running atop drums and rollers. It must have looked gangly and awkward, like a freight car on a leash, as everyone became silent. It was September 22, 1845. With a crowd of eight hundred looking on, the engine shuddered and smoked, its stationary feet ripping into the black, buckling turf. Then the ropes whined, and the Satellite lurched.

•

Between the 1820s and the 1850s, a new kind of existence came into view, powered not by lumbering bodies but by gravity and coal. The fusion of philosophical idealism with innovations in mechanics released a soaring optimism. Go back to 1750, and everyone on earth lived nearly the same way— moving only as fast as a horse, pulling only as much as an ox, and preparing food, shelter, and clothing by hand. It was a biological old regime about to be overthrown. In 1814 the industrial advocate Tench Coxe reported statistics meant to dazzle Americans. With the British technology of the time, Coxe said, 100,000 Americans (roughly the population of Baltimore) could mill as much cotton into yarn as eight million people (the entire population of the United States in 1810) could accomplish by hand in the same amount of time. The outlines of a new economy became distinctive even as it remained firmly anchored to the larger economy of nature. Anyone who had ever felt his teeth rattle in his head as hundreds of looms shook the beams and floors of a water-powered factory—as it turned out bolts of cloth like eggs from an automated henhouse—walked away thinking that the human economy no longer possessed definite limits. Material progress did not first appear in the 1820s, but only then did many people witness its possibilities; only then did they really experience it. According to anthropologist Ernest Gellner, "A society had now emerged which, for the very first time in history, was based on sustained, perpetual cognitive and economic growth."[2]

Economic growth is a measure of *throughput*, or the capacity of a system to transfer raw material from environments to consumers through a widening process of production. Growth thrives where proliferating needs meet proliferating means. It creates webs of consumption, as when people clear land to produce corn to feed cattle to turn out beef and leather to make car seats for Cadillac Escalades. All along the line the demand for additional fuel, labor, housing, food, medical care, and roads contributes to that great measure of prosperity—GDP. Growth is also impelled by capitalism, a system of organizing labor and land that creates *capital*. Capital is the profit or surplus value resulting from production that is then reinvested in technology or additional labor to increase production, creating still more surplus value. This never-ending necessity to keep all the factors of production fully employed makes capitalism different from any other economic system that has ever existed. Adam Smith bluntly asserted that no rational person would behave any other way: "A man must be perfectly crazy who, where there is tolerable security, does not employ all the stock which he commands." Anyone in the possession of capital, wrote Smith, "always expects it to be replaced to him with a profit." Karl Marx shouted out this imperative, this drive to expand: "Accumulate, accumulate! That is Moses and the prophets! . . . Accumulation for the sake of accumulation, production for the sake of production."[3] The self-perpetuating cycle of accumulation has absorbed nearly the entire material world, turning everything into a commodity.

But while growth has existed, in some sense, for as long as the human population has been increasing, its identification with *progress*—a human value—is more recent. The word dates to 1475, but its usage took a noticeable turn with the publication of *The Pilgrim's Progress: From This World to That Which Is to Come* (1678). John Bunyan's allegory follows the life of Christian as he navigates a treacherous moral universe, avoiding a gauntlet of shady characters. Christian visits the Palace of Deliverance, climbs the Hill of Difficulty, passes through the Valley of the Shadow of Death, and finally makes it to the Celestial City. Before Bunyan, progress mostly referred to movement across a landscape or through the country. After Bunyan, it referred to the movement of the soul through the labyrinth of society to the sacred geography of heaven. The sense of movement took on moral direction. Progress didn't simply get one from place to place, it represented betterment, improvement, as one moved closer to the goal of salvation by overcoming the moral obstacles of life. For centuries, the natural environment had no particular role to play in salvation, but that was about to change.

Then came the Enlightenment. Radical thinkers, including Francis Bacon, René Descartes, and Baruch Spinoza, argued that the world could be understood by experience, without reference to God. By arguing that God was the inner essence of all things and not their direct cause, Spinoza equated God with Nature, as having no personality, no conscious power, and no independent control over human affairs. Spinoza ripped a hole in the keel of the old-time religion, and nature came pouring in. Nature quickly emerged as the new foundation of the social order. It could be observed; its properties could be demonstrated; and its vastness lent eternal and self-evident truth to just about anything. So John Locke asserted that a primordial "state of nature" established "natural rights," and Thomas Jefferson claimed the rightful independence of the United States by appealing to "the Laws of Nature and of Nature's God." Adam Smith, author of *The*

Wealth of Nations (1776), did not see God directing people toward their best interests when he devised the "invisible hand," but some unnamed force, comparable to gravity. God ceased to be the King of Kings and became more like a constitutional monarch, following earthly rules. As for the destiny of the soul in heaven, it came to be replaced by human destiny as the material world took on greater importance: as people understood it better, manipulated it on a larger scale, and saw it as a way to wealth.

Progress became material. Social observers ceased to refer to God at all in their attempts to relate the story of civilization. The philosophers of the Scottish Enlightenment, including Adam Ferguson, David Hume, Lord Kames, and Adam Smith, introduced a story meant to sync with the Bible and supersede every chronicle of kings and ministers, to reveal the primal motives and environmental influences behind human history. We all know how it goes. In the beginning, there were poor savages who never accumulated enough food by hunting and gathering to sustain more than a few wretched people in scattered groups. Finally using their wits to escape their pitiful starvation, they captured horses and domesticated sheep, living as shepherds or (in the action-thriller version) as pillaging barbarians. Population increased to the point where wild forage became scarce, making it necessary for people to stay in one place and cultivate some of the large-seeded grasses their sheep had been gnawing on for millennia. Farmers produced more food than hunters or pastoralists, resulting in more births. Their surplus grain and milk could be traded in villages, sustaining a population of nonproducers, including princes, bureaucrats, soldiers, and merchants. Divisions of labor, rule by law, a free and open market, great commercial cities—all these defined "civil society"—the final stage of social evolution.[4] Progress in the final stage took a different form than it had before: constant expansion. Society would never again evolve into something else; it would just get bigger and bigger, adding new markets, new territory, and more people into its benevolent vortex.

The theory of stages presented the way things must have happened, probably happened, should have happened. Its central assumption, that history has direction and meaning, originated with the messianic faith of the Torah and the New Testament. The narrative translated that faith into secular terms. It built a bridge between religious destiny and the new materialism. It redefined salvation as deliverance from dearth and hunger at the savage edge of subsistence, fulfilling God's Providence with a set of human institutions that mediated the attainment of necessary things.[5] The soul ends up not in the Celestial City, but in the city of shopkeepers. Material progress differed from salvation in another way. It must not end. "If progress is not made," wrote the Scottish historian James Dunbar in 1780, "we must decline from the good state already attained." Edward Everett, as governor of Massachusetts, gave an extraordinary speech in 1840 in which he intoned, "The progress which has been made in art and science is, indeed, vast. We are ready to think . . . that the goal must be at hand. But there is no goal; and there can be no pause; for art and science are, in themselves, progressive and infinite . . . Nothing can arrest them which does not plunge the entire order of society into barbarism."[6] Everett was very clear. Any pause would result in a terrifying regression, a falling back from plenty and refinement into the strife and violence of the past.

The absence of a distinct goal allowed advocates of material progress to project their expectations onto the future. It gave economic growth its indeterminate quality and captured the imagination of social thinkers who began to maintain that under certain circumstances, nations could achieve sustained affluence. The phrase "national wealth" appeared for the first time in 1680, when political economist William Petyt wrote, "It is evident that all sorts of home manufactures must advance or save the National Wealth." Smith said that growth had been going on for more than a century by the time he noticed it; in fact, "since the time of Henry VIII the wealth and revenue of the country have been continually advancing . . . They seem, not only to have been going on, but to have been going on faster and faster." Adam Ferguson believed that the advance of revenue had no clear beginning and no terminus: "The materials of human art are never entirely exhausted," he wrote in 1767, "and the applications of industry are never at an end." By the middle of the next century, with steam engines harnessed and hissing in every major American town, possibility became expectation. Industrial throughput and the terrific returns from overseas colonies gave intellectuals of every designation a view from the mountaintop. As one utopian leader wrote in 1840, "Man . . . seeks for happiness and enjoyment as a law of his nature, as a part of his destiny;—he seeks for riches and the goods of this earth, as a right." Etzler simply described the going trend: "The mass of the civilized nations turn their minds now more to the earthly improvements of life."[7]

Things came together. An older metaphysical progress married a burgeoning productive capacity, creating a powerful ideology of growth—driven by the myth of human perfection and grounded in the precise observation of economic reality.

Etzler is a nexus for the complex of ideas that boiled and simmered into a full-fledged conception of material progress. He was not a major theorist. He did not invent anything we use today. But we can read him to understand the practical and utopian aspects of economic growth in the Atlantic economy of the nineteenth century. He sounded like any political economist when he proposed to use "the materials of the world to the best purpose of human life, as the true universal means of the salvation of all mankind, not in dreams, but in the plain realities of life . . . food, clothing, houses, comforts, and conveniences."[8] He sounded like any engineer when he noted that "powers must pre-exist. They cannot be invented . . . no mechanism can produce power." He anticipated the possible: "There is nothing in my proposals that the Americans do not practice already, nothing new, but the objects themselves to be attained." There is something deeply pragmatic about Etzler's schemes and something fundamentally utopian about economic growth, and vice versa. They share the same qualities, and Etzler illuminates them and almost every important materialist idea during the time in which he lived.

In its open-ended promises and totalizing patterns, the Satellite is an emblem of our own assumptions. Etzler's life and thought illustrate a conception of nature and society that, although eccentric—coming from one who believed that the earth would one day support a population of one trillion people—is oddly familiar. For as much as we tend to dismiss utopia for the way it wishes away greed and poverty, we would do well to consider the ways that the North American Free Trade Agreement, the Mall of America, and the Williams-Sonoma catalog partake of the very same expectation of salvation. What happens when we read plenty into environments that have the same kinds of limits our own bodies do? What does it mean that wealth in capitalist societies must be thought of as endless if the system is to avoid contradictions that might destroy it? What was Etzler trying to create with the Satellite and a colony in Venezuela that shows us a picture of ourselves? The following is Etzler's story, but it is also a journey through nineteenth-century materialism, through the scientific, economic, and geographical thinking that created his context and made idealist engineering seem plausible. That such a thing ever existed suggests what lies ahead in this book. Discoveries in the physical world gave hope to some that the Celestial City might be built, that Eden might be planted.

At Satellite Field, the crowd turned away drunk and drowsy after the chief engineer released the steam from the boiler in the late afternoon. They'd seen locomotives move at forty miles per hour, so why all the fuss over an overwrought plow? (Some said they'd have rather seen a good fight.) No one disputed that the Satellite, moving at less than three miles per hour, plowed up eighty acres over three days, but the members of the Tropical Emigration Society argued for years about what actually happened in that field. Stollmeyer declared the machine's modest performance a success, proof that the Satellite had opened a long-hidden passageway in human progress. *Lloyd's Weekly* gave a cooler assessment. The test established "a new mechanical principle . . . the transmission of power from a fixed point to a moving point, going in arbitrary directions at the will of one man at the steering wheel, which was thought impossible by scientific engineers." Those among Etzler's faithful who expected something miraculous to happen recommitted themselves to the colony in Venezuela as their best chance to discover lifelong ease and abundance. As for Etzler, not even Stollmeyer knew exactly where he was, and though the society managed to fill the columns in *The Morning Star* reserved for his dispatches, these came irregularly. As fissures opened up around Stollmeyer, he felt compelled to defend the machine as well as its inventor.

•

John Adolphus Etzler (born Johann Adolph) grew up in Mühlhausen, in the central German state of Thüringen, on the River Unstrut. An even plain of fields rising into gentle forested hills surrounds the city. Tree-lined canals run from the river throughout the plain and suggest that a once-marshy landscape had been reclaimed into a more highly ordered one. Here the Protestant radical Thomas Müntzer roused peasants to revolt against their feudal lords in 1524. He claimed few allies, least of all his former teacher, Martin Luther, who called for his execution. One year later, in the battle of Frankenhausen, Müntzer led a force of eight thousand in a desperate tactic to weaken the hold of entrenched landed authority. Victorious lords dragged the insurgent to the public square and beheaded him. In 1707 Johann Sebastian Bach accepted a position as organist in the church of the Divi Blasii and there composed *A Fixed Mountain Is Our God* and the Prelude and Fugue in G Minor—two of his church cantatas.[9] Etzler's father, David Christoph Etzler, worked as a shoemaker and married Maria Christina Fröbe in 1790 at the altar of the Divi Blasii. Born February 22, 1791, the oldest of Maria and David's seven children, Johann would have observed holy days in the cathedral's Gothic nave, hearing music produced by forced air though pipes of varying widths and lengths, as the sun reached his face through a rose-petal window twenty feet wide.

David worked from a shop at home while young Johann collected the awls, round knives, mallets, and forms of the cobbler's box. The child would have been expected to enter his father's trade, but David died in 1808 at the age of forty-eight, when Johann was seventeen.[10] By then, Etzler had been thoroughly trained as a tradesman, but he also prepared as a scholar at the town *Gymnasium* (high school), where he learned engineering as part of a curriculum that stressed worldly needs and the betterment of the *Heimat*—the homeland or town. At school he might have used the *Kleiner Schul-Atlas* (1806), which explains such mysteries of geography as the seasonal position of the earth as it orbits the sun. The Louisiana Territory is indicated, along with New Granada, a vast Spanish colony that by 1806 had become a single viceroyalty comprising Panama, Colombia, Ecuador, and Venezuela.

One of Etzler's greatest influences might have been the one he witnessed in the landscape. Gottfried Tulla, perhaps the most talented and ambitious engineer in Europe, spent the year 1791 studying hydrology in the Netherlands, where he first imagined controlling the floodplain of the Rhine. Germans had sought that control for centuries, trying every- thing to restrict the river's highly variable seasonal flow in or- der to keep marshes and fens in permanent cultivation. Etzler came of age in the midst of this revolution, during the years in which Tulla succeeded in confining the upper river within an artificial bed. The engineer tamed the Rhine by perform- ing miracles of earthen matter. He shortened it by straighten- ing its meandering course; he opened it to more rapid commerce by scraping away more than twenty-two hundred islands; he disciplined the river by constructing 160 miles of dikes, requiring 6.5 million yards of earth. The Erie Canal looks like a barnyard trench compared with what Tulla did to the Rhine. It must have made an impression on Etzler. It said that engineering—a practical physics dedicated to social im- provement—could reconfigure marshland and floodplains into territory profitable, inhabitable, and cultivated. The canals of Mühlhausen probably date from the same era of reclamation and state formation.[11]

Etzler's schoolmates were a technically talented genera- tion, including the composers Ernst and Adolph Methfessel, the architect Friedrich August Stüler (who designed the Na- tional Gallery in Berlin), and Johann August Röbling (John Augustus Roebling)—the future designer of the Brooklyn

Bridge—who shared with Etzler an interest in engineering and philosophy. After *Gymnasium*, Roebling enrolled in the Royal Polytechnic Institute (now the Technical University of Berlin), graduating in 1826. If Etzler attended university, he would have graduated years earlier, being fifteen years older than Roebling, but there is no documented enrollment for Etzler at either the Royal Polytechnic Institute or the University of Berlin. How Etzler spent the years from 1810 to 1822, when he turned thirty-one, is impossible to know, but with his father gone, he undoubtedly shared the burden of earning an income to keep his mother and younger siblings under a roof. He might have worked as an engineer on one of the reclamation projects. We know from Roebling that Etzler boarded a ship for the United States in 1822 and spent the next seven years there, probably in Pennsylvania.

Etzler recorded nothing of these years, and no one recorded anything of him. But it's clear what he was thinking. A liberal aristocrat observing the emigration of young men like Etzler wrote *Der Deutsche in Nord-Amerika* (1818), a kind of manual to guide the morals of idealists on the move. "You shall and will devote yourself *to the service of the human race*, and of your poor countrymen," the book instructed, "and if destiny has precluded you from exerting in other ways a beneficial influence on the *fortunes of the nations*, your spirit may find its compensation in this."[12] German conservatives showed nothing but disdain for the emigrants of the 1820s, dismissing them as "political malcontents." Seekers such as Etzler found a model in George Rapp, a liberal pietist from Württemberg who broke with the Lutheran Church in 1798 and fled to Butler County, Pennsylvania, where in 1804 he founded the commune of Harmonie.[13] Rapp preached that Jesus would return in his lifetime, but had trouble deciding exactly where he and his followers needed to be when the miracle happened. He moved his flock to Indiana in 1814, founding another Harmonie, and then back to Pennsylvania, founding Economy. It is possible that Etzler joined Rapp's community somewhere along the way.

Etzler returned to Mühlhausen in 1829 not because he had failed in America, but because he wanted to convince others to follow him back. He fell into a cauldron of reactionary politics. While he was away, the German aristocracy had moved to dam up the foreign influence leaking through its western border. The youth had become smitten with French enthusiasm, French politics, and even French fashion—openly claiming that these spoke for freedom from arbitrary rule. Students in the universities and high schools wanted some form of democracy, but the Prussian state would have none of it. The liberal historian Carl von Rotteck, himself a victim of the reaction, described the fermentation in Germany after the Napoleonic Wars as a "general feeling of *unwell-being*." Rotteck saw a nation caught between "the continuance of the vexations of the old, and the non-appearance of the promised benefits of the new . . . a nation awakened in the war of liberation to thoughts of liberty."[14] Dismissive of the explosive force they had bottled up, the aristocracy made it illegal for members of the educated class to emigrate, especially those with technical knowledge. It was the most intense period of religious and philosophical conflict in Germany since the Reformation.

Etzler risked his life by openly advocating emigration to the United States in order to save a generation of thinkers from stagnation and paralysis under the heel of a lame yet still dangerous aristocracy. Imagine him standing in the streets of Mühlhausen, clothed in the same reeking coat he wore in the hold during the passage, gaunt and bearded, secretly conspiring with artisans, preaching about Pennsylvania to anyone who would listen. An English follower of the 1840s gave the only known description of him as being "below the middle stature, but of a firmly knit and muscular frame," with a "massy" head, a large, protruding brow, and a countenance "more of the intellect than of the feelings." Etzler's broad face, rounded chin, blue eyes, and wide mouth lent him a "habitual sternness of expression." The observer watched him speak to a crowd, "grasping the floor with his foot, his head thrown back, his broad chest advanced—firm and motionless."[15] He threw logic; he demanded attention; he spoke treason. To the hushed folk of Mühlhausen he must have seemed as threatening in his own way as stocky Thomas Müntzer, and he strained to hold the same ground where Müntzer spilled his blood. Prussian police arrested the street rat without a warrant and threw him in jail.

Rotting in the hulk gave physical metaphor to the impossible contradiction between the freedom of his spirit and the bleak medal-chested bureaucracy of King Frederick William III. In those moments, Etzler might have meditated on the apostle of freedom, the enthralling and aloof figure who dominated intellectual life in Germany—Georg Wilhelm Friedrich Hegel.

In 1818 Hegel emerged as the leading intellectual in Germany, accepting the chair in philosophy at the University of Berlin—the most visible academic position in the philosophical world. He wielded unprecedented influence. A generation of Germans came to him, and he gave them new tools for contemplating thought and consciousness, for seeking new meaning in politics and history. Philosophers as far back as Plato described ideas and social structures as eternal, the truth as unchanging. Hegel blew that to bits and ignited his audience: everything is becoming, emerging, evolving through the winnowing process of historical conflict and the development of mind. He handed his students a kind of X-ray vision for seeing the world without its totalitarian offices, without the weight of custom, a world in which history had direction and culmination without God pulling the strings. He spoke of the contradictions of modern life, of the "conflict between what is and what ought to be."[16] He told them things about the moral and material world that they desperately wanted to believe—that "all the qualities of Spirit exist only through Freedom; that all are but means for attaining Freedom." Hegel imagined a just state, one that expressed reason and embodied liberty. He said that Germans could be a world-historical people, with the strength of Spirit (mind) to bring on the culmination of history.[17] And he moved students to seek his ideals in the world. As abstract and inward as the philosophy might seem, it actually impelled its followers outward.

Students nearly dedicated their lives to Hegel. They mobbed his lectures, straining the baffled police to keep order. One of the old guard described students "driven in crowds into Hegel's colleges." They worked harder listening to Hegel than they did reading him. One of Hegel's most devoted admirers, Heinrich Gustav Hotho, recorded the Master's halting style—how he hacked and coughed, stopped to swallow in the middle of sentences, and generally struggled to get a word out (the "birth-labor of thought," as Hotho put it). But the audience was enthralled, and Hotho recalled, "I felt myself irresistibly bound to him . . . So completely did all previous ways of thinking vanish." An American commentator said that Hegelianism shaped the education of the German elite: "The prevalent system of philosophy in Germany is that of Hegel . . . It is, in short, the form in which the German mind now exists."[18] The ferment did not dissipate with Hegel's death. He spawned a generation of

Hegel, the philosophical mentor to a generation of thinkers. Hegel's teach-
ings impelled his students outward to discover rationality in the world. He
certainly did not invent economic growth, but by declaring that nature
served philosophical ends and that all progress began with thought, he put
forward an idealism that lacked any tether to material reality. Portrait
of Hegel (1831) by Johann Jakob Schlesinger, Nationalgalerie, Staatliche
Museen zu Berlin. (Courtesy Bildarchiv Preussischer Kulturbesitz/Art Resource)

Young Hegelians, including Ludwig Feuerbach and Karl
Marx. The expansiveness of his thought made it possible to
carve many possible positions from it. According to one recent interpreter, "Hegel's philosophy was something that social and political radicals, discontented with the existing order
of things, could use for their own purpose." The young Marx
wrote to his father in November 1837, thrilled by his reading
of a philosopher who embraced the overarching problem of
history and society, the conflict between "what is and what
ought to be."

Hegel's philosophy unwinds like a spiral. Every paragraph

expresses the central idea of the entire system. The universe is rational, and people have the capacity to understand nature and history because the order of the human mind replicates the order of the universe. Hegel said that rationality exists absolutely, not as some figment or illusion: "The real is the rational and the rational is the real." Rationality also described a process of becoming, of emerging. He theorized that history continually resolved social and political contradictions: master and slave, revolution and reaction. For Hegel, history moved through an epic series of conflicts, producing resolutions that contained within them new conflicts.[19] He called this the dialectic, and because everything in the universe exhibited the same rationality—from the orbit of the planets to the alignment of the soul—the dialectic could be understood both as a kind of law of nature and as a method of thinking. For Hegel, all lines ran parallel, with thought and history—in fact, everything in existence—pointing toward the same fantastic culmination in absolute freedom, absolute knowledge, and absolute goodness. But history would not culminate all by itself, and this is where every one of Hegel's students held his breath. The awakening of a nation required struggle. Freedom had to be won, morality established, truths discovered. Yet progress in human events had no certain place for nature.

Hegel was not a Romantic in the mold of the poets and painters associated with the English and American movement. Think of William Wordsworth's quiet contemplation of the Lake District and Thomas Cole's luminous canvases of the Hudson River Valley. Hegel didn't find truth in nature. To the extent that he wrote about the natural environment at all, he saw it as brute matter to be transformed by Spirit: "Nature confronts us as a riddle and a problem, whose solution both attracts and repels us: attracts us, because Spirit is presaged in Nature; repels us, because Nature seems an alien existence . . . Whatever forces Nature develops and lets loose against man—cold, wild beasts, water, fire—he knows means to counter them . . . The cunning of his reason enables him to preserve and maintain himself in face of the forces of Nature." Humans could morally regard what they found in environments as *means*, not *ends*: "Since it is *our* end which is paramount, not natural things themselves, we convert the latter into means, the destiny of which is determined by us, not by the things themselves."[20]

This was not something Hegel fretted about; no dialectic wrestled fitfully to be resolved. He found living things boring. They followed predictable laws, did the same things over and over in self-repeating cycles, never developed into anything new, and so could never lead to the perfectibility of society. "In Nature," he wrote, "there happens 'nothing new under the sun,' and the multiform play of its phenomena so far induces a feeling of ennui." Only changes that took place within the region of the Spirit, under the force of rationality, produced change. "This peculiarity in the world of mind has indicated in the case of man an altogether different destiny from that of merely natural objects . . . namely, a real capacity for change, and that for the better,—an impulse of *perfectibility*."[21] At the same time that other intellectuals reveled on craggy mountaintops in rejection of commodities and capitalism, Hegel did not waver from human goals and aspirations. This is the other idealism—the one that insisted on a progressive humanity over-against (to use a German expression) the capacities of nature. Hegel probably did not influence many American or English political economists, nor did many industrialists link themselves to his thought, but every economic thinker and businessman before mid-century had one thing in common with Hegel: by rendering nature dead and directionless, they could read into it their own meta-narrative, one that enshrined expansion as the way to universal peace and happiness. So conceived, human progress had no use for actual environments consisting of actual organisms living in actual time, yet this is the idealism that filled capitalism with metaphysical inspiration.

In the 1830s Marx and other Young Hegelians wanted to apply Hegel to the real world, especially Hegel's tantalizing claim that Spirit produced Being. The group included Ludwig Feuerbach, whose *Essence of Christianity* (1841) exploded over the intellectual landscape of Europe. Where Hegel treated the material world as emerging from the sensations of thought, Feuerbach flipped the Master: for Feuerbach, thought emerged from the material world. "One knows the man by the object that reflects his being; the object lets his being appear to you; the object is his manifest being." If the way we see the world is directly caused by our material existence—by our social class, by how we consume, by the things we own—then a change in our condition would change our view of reality. This is the entrance to materialism, the notion that physical existence is the basis of reality and that social relations have material causes. Marx could hardly catch his breath after reading Feuerbach: "There are moments when philosophy turns its eyes to the external world, and no longer apprehends it, but, as a practical person, weaves, as it were, intrigues with the world . . . The same now with the philosophy of Hegel." This is what Marx meant when he said, "Philosophy has become worldly."[22]

Five years later, in *The German Ideology*, Marx unveiled the consummate materialism—the pivotal moment in his transition from idealist philosopher to radical political economist: "As individuals express their life, so they are. What they are, therefore, coincides with what they produce, with *what* they produce and *how* they produce. The nature of individuals thus depends on the material conditions which determine their production." Marx became such a firebrand that it is easy to lose sight of his philosophical accomplishments. We are all followers of Marx in the sense that we all believe that the way people view the world is heavily influenced by their material means. It wouldn't be surprising to find out that a corporate CEO believes that the government reflects her interests when her campaign contributions buy her a breakfast meeting with members of Congress. Now consider a minimum-wage earner who can't make the rent or pay insurance on a car. How might she define citizenship differently? Advocates of economic growth embrace that kind of materialism wholeheartedly, adding that it is possible to change the way people think about themselves and their role in society by increasing their incomes.[23] Materialism can be overwrought. It can undervalue religion and culture, missing important factors in social change. But for the analysis it made possible, it stands as a remarkable accomplishment.

Etzler moved in the same direction as Marx and Feuerbach (though there is no indication that he knew the work of either) to derive Spirit from Being, a new social life from transformations in the uses and quantities of energy. The literalness of his paradise posited a relationship between the environment and the way people thought, felt, and behaved. Beauty and abundance would eliminate crime and even deceit. Health and convenience would banish irony. Etzler would have surely agreed with Marx that "the standpoint of the old materialism is civil society; the standpoint of the new is human society, or social humanity."[24] The old materialism stressed individuals acting to maximize their self-interest in a system that left them isolated, empty, dependent. The new materialism, as Etzler and Marx saw it, began with a universal social vision and a scientific understanding of nature. But unlike Marx, Etzler imagined away all limits by claiming that nature never ceased to provide for the improvement of the human condition. This view characterized the thinking of capitalists as well. Idealizing the capacity of nature as a prelude to any economic theory became a common way of speaking and writing in the nineteenth century, as all kinds of people tried to comprehend the promise of modernity.

•

Etzler had Hegel to mull over when jailers brought his daily gruel. In calling for Germans to leave the fatherland and join him in the United States, he lived out another facet of Hegel's philosophy—the belief that "America is . . . the land of the future, where, in the ages that lie before us, the burden of the World's History shall reveal itself."[25] Hegel argued that history had a geographical basis and that North America provided the best evidence. The Spirit of a people germinates from the particular conditions of their land, their environment. "This character is nothing more or less than the mode and form in which nations make their appearance in History." No world-historical people could come from either the frigid or torrid zones, said Hegel, only from the temperate climates. Rotteck called the United States an "asylum of all the victims of foreign oppression." But conservatives, like Wolfgang Menzel, decried transatlantic emigration as betrayal: "Thus are Germans fruitlessly scattered far and wide over the face of the globe." Menzel suggested that young men ramble up the Danube into frontiers that Germany could claim for her own, to "increase her external strength and extend her influence," as though the discontented would serve as vanguard troops for the very state they despised.[26]

Released in 1830, grossly dissatisfied with the life he

faced, Etzler ran into Roebling. They must have had light coming out of their eyes. The tumult surrounding them seemed ordered up by Hegel to resolve the contradictions of the age into a new historical moment. Roebling had known Hegel in Berlin, had become a visitor to the professor's home and taken walks with him. In the shadow of his mentor, Roebling had prepared his own philosophical manuscript, yet he had no outlet, no territory where his idealism might flourish. He had qualified to practice bridge design at the age of fourteen, and he looked forward to some kind of career as a civil engineer.[27] By law, he owed the state two years of service following graduation; after that, he might have taken the deal offered him, working the rest of his life on a government salary for the Prussian railroad. Bored and pent up, he listened as Etzler told him about Pennsylvania. Together, the two printed a pamphlet, which they distributed secretly, *A General View of the United States of North America, Together with a Community Plan for Settlement*, most of it written by Etzler. Roebling then organized an emigration society and drew up an underground plan for escape.

In 1831, everyone seemed to be searching.[28] In May, Alexis de Tocqueville and Gustave Beaumont arrived in New York to begin a tour of the United States. Nat Turner's slave rebellion began in August; his death followed in November. Cyrus McCormick invented the reaping machine. The John Bull, the first steam-driven railroad locomotive, arrived from England for service on the Camden and Amboy Railroad in New Jersey. Charles Darwin embarked on the HMS *Beagle*— the journey that would result in the theory of evolution. Most momentous to Etzler and Roebling, the July Revolution had begun in France in 1830, filling Europe with a sense of panic and insecurity. The leading powers moved to stabilize the continent after more than two decades of war and revolution, but with every move they managed only to intensify the rebellion. Many recalled the grand affair of state that took place in 1814, a meeting some called the Congress of Vienna and others a conspiracy to undermine the principles of the French Revolution. In what must be the most inflammatory policy ever adopted by an international body, the ministers agreed to restore the Bourbons—the old French monarchy—the same family that was violently deposed in 1792. By 1830, the Bourbon king Charles X flaunted his plan to bring back the French nobility and caused citizens to grind their teeth by his treading on the memory of the Revolution itself, even denigrating the tricolor banner.

The revolt that followed brought the final downfall of the Bourbons and spread a sense of change that, though it blew past Germany in 1789, now contributed to the cause against the government. The liberal historian Rotteck coolly observed, "The edifice of a new European order, built up artfully, finely and self-pleasingly, by the diplomatic architects of the Congress of Vienna, was shaken in all its joints." One policy after another fell "to the rocking foundations." In the state of Aachen, citizens raised the tricolor in solidarity with the French. Bread riots and the burning of manorial records and government offices took place in Kessel, just forty miles west of Mühlhausen. A spontaneous congress in Dresden published a constitution modeled on the Declaration of the Rights of Man, proclaiming the people sovereign, the nobility abolished, and the army dissolved. Armed and in the streets, citizens prepared to smash the government "with the butt-ends of our guns." Terrified government troops opened fire to disperse the crowds.[29] Just before Hegel's death (another of the foreboding events of 1831), he spoke of the July Revolution as "a crisis in which everything that was formally valid seemed to have become problematical." In the words of one historian, the men and women who faced and then escaped revolution shared certain qualities: "austerely moral, fervently patriotic, and imbued . . . with an idealism that cared little for actual conditions, but was quite willing to reconstruct the world anew according to a preconceived notion."[30] The July Revolution caused them such agony because it lacked the heat and kindling necessary to incinerate the old regime.

The members of Roebling's emigration society chartered the *Henry Barclay* for a passage to Philadelphia. Roebling and his brother Carl, along with forty-three other seekers, set out in May. But when they arrived at the port of Bremen, they found that 230 men, women, and children from the town of Darmstadt, a group that was to unite with Roebling's for the crossing, had sailed the day before—for Baltimore. A few days later, the contingent from Mühlhausen arrived, including Etzler and perhaps seventy others. They paid for tickets aboard the *August Edward*, traveling steerage from Bremen on May 23 for a voyage lasting eleven weeks. They ate bacon, beans, grits, coffee, sauerkraut, and black bread. Each passenger received a hogshead of water in a daily ration. They squinted into the glary horizon, tended to the sick in the dank hold, and slept together in a heap. Roebling liked to stand at the bowsprit looking down at the hypnotic motion—how the ship, "driven by the tensely swelled sails, makes its way by main force through the on-rushing billows." Roebling imagined himself a great leader who would found a society of heroically philosophical Germans somewhere in the American South, but the early departure of the Darmstadt group had deflated him. He penned a long letter about his journey and rethought his plan toward a smaller settlement in the North. Etzler kept to himself. At night, in the candlelit hold, he too felt the incessant motion of the vessel. A health inspector boarded the ship at anchorage in Delaware Bay on August 6, and the company entered Philadelphia the same day, bounding off the wharf with their wool caps and their pipes—dead-on signs, wrote Roebling, of German immigrants. Americans wore straw or felt hats and smoked cigars.[31]

The two groups never reunited. The passengers aboard the *Henry Barclay* bickered and split up while at sea. No longer huddled together against the authorities, they discovered their divisions. Some went off to join George Rapp's settlement in Indiana, though by then Rapp had returned to Pennsylvania after selling the place to Robert Owen. The others scattered. Fissures in Roebling's group also opened. He described one passenger as "a spoiled city man," others as having "exaggerated and romantic ideas," still others as incompetent and "of little value." He and Etzler originally planned to take the company to west Florida, but Nat Turner's rebellion of that year turned them against the idea. Roebling learned that in the South, "no individual can undertake anything without considerable property." The company would have been subject to prosecution had they attempted to educate slaves or treat them as equals.[32]

Instead, Roebling recommitted himself to establishing a farm or village, and this led to a falling-out with his old friend. Etzler bridled under the oppressive blandness of the scheme. A farm would only replicate the same slavish life, dull customs, social relations, and constant labor that he wanted to transform. He had become aloof and uncooperative, wanting to lead his own company into some vastly different venture. Writing home, Roebling explained why he sought to separate from a small number who allied themselves with Etzler: "From our longer association with these people only disadvantage and not advantage could result, both in pecuniary and social relations. Etzler would have brought us only disadvantage, no advantage; he demands only more sacrifices from our side after we had already sacrificed enough; and what was even more annoying, he demanded that every man should subordinate himself to his views, which we did not like to do." Seven men broke off with Etzler. Roebling dismissed them, after weighing what damage their absence might cause the project: "All these people possess few means and little education." One spat back over his shoulder, "Etzler is leading the people to their higher life's happiness." Then they were gone.

The feeling of vacancy stayed with Roebling for some time, and he complained, "Not one of these people took leave of us, and only Etzler wrote me a letter composed in a friendly but somewhat mystic tone." He put down his feelings in a long letter, explaining what Etzler had once meant to him: "I still respect Etzler and have the best opinion of his mind and heart, only he has too stubborn a head, offends all the world, is not a businessman, not in the least, and he does not know how to ingratiate himself with people or how to behave toward them." Roebling assessed his old friend as being "capable of everything good," but perhaps not of forming a community "because of his stubbornness and his awkward and objectionable manner." The two differed in temperament, but they shared the same certainty that the world promised more than what existed—that the possible was actual. Roebling predicted that when the competition, strife, and jealousy between nations finally ended, people would join together to do marvelous things: plant the African deserts, defeat "mosquitoes and alligators," and perform massive works, like sinking wells a thousand feet deep in order to irrigate forests in the Great Basin. A unified humanity would transform everything to make the earth itself richer, fuller.

Roebling never saw Etzler again. Years later, Washington Roebling wrote about Etzler, "My father considered him the greatest genius he ever met."[33]

Of the three hundred people who joined the group, only Roebling's two brothers and the seven indentured members of the Grabe family founded the colony of Saxonburg in Butler County, twenty-five miles from Pittsburgh. Roebling purchased seven thousand acres that once belonged to Robert Morris, a member of the Continental Congress and later a senator from Pennsylvania and secretary of the treasury. Morris had assembled it from land taken directly from Indians and from the warrants issued to soldiers after the Revolution. Other settlers soon arrived from Germany, and an 1835 woodcut of the village makes it appear modestly prosperous. On summer nights they drank rye whiskey and danced in the heat. Roebling worked the farm and village for six years, growing ever more bored with it. He fiddled with boilers to see if he could invent a more accurate heat gauge to prevent explosions. He applied for a patent for a machine somewhat similar to the Satellite in its functions—a steam-driven tractor/plow/reaper. He invented a "radial engine" that would operate at intense heat.

In 1837 Roebling went to work as an assistant engineer on the Sandy and Beaver branch of the Pennsylvania Canal and, after that, as a surveyor for the Pennsylvania Railroad during the construction of its route over the Allegheny Mountains, from Harrisburg to Pittsburgh. That's when he first saw the portage railways connecting sections of the canal that had been separated by mountain ranges. Ropes of nine-inch-thick Kentucky hemp pulled boats and railcars up these inclined planes, and the ropes sometimes shredded and snapped. One day he watched helplessly as a runaway car crushed two men to death. The solution went off in his head

Saxonburg, 1835. Etzler rejected Roebling's village and never spent a day there. (Special Collections and University Archives, Rutgers University Libraries)

like a detonator: *wire rope*. It combined the increasingly common use of steel for building with the circumstantial demands of the inclined plane; it was stronger than hemp and might be of use in bridge design. In 1841 he began to manufacture wire rope at Saxonburg—a practical innovation that made possible the realization of a great Hegelian project, a bridge anchored in the earth but suspended in air, a kind of dialectic in stone and steel.[34]

Etzler and the separatists left on the road in the direction of Pittsburgh. A Mr. Kleber met Etzler's party on a steamboat up the Ohio River, but without Etzler, who had left with another man to scout out land in Ohio and Indiana. Finding none to his liking or that he could afford, Etzler showed up in Cincinnati, most likely joining the community of Young Hegelians who sought out the city for its proximity to the uncharted West. A letter dated September 3, 1832, arrived at Rapp's third settlement, Economy. In it, Etzler asked for a line of credit and insisted that rumors about him as a fraud and con artist were lies.[35] Rapp became crucial to Etzler's plans; the old utopian represented something of the

pragmatic idealism that Etzler would soon test with his books
and inventions and the kind of community of enlightened
Germans that he hoped to found himself. In effect, Etzler
wanted Rapp to finance his schemes—perhaps Etzler's way of
gaining legitimacy from Rapp's reputation. As a sign of his
independence from his would-be mentor, Etzler never joined
Economy. But he hung around long enough to witness a
challenge to Rapp from a bizarre interloper.

One day in 1833, a man calling himself Count Maximilian
of Leon walked into Economy. Count Leon—self-proclaimed
Anointed of God, Stem of Judah, and Root of David—offered
a salvation even more quick and easy than Rapp's (who set
the date for the arrival of the New Jerusalem in 1836). It says
something about the heightened messianic expectation of
Rapp's followers that perhaps as many as a third of them
dropped tools and followed the "Count" across the Beaver
River to an eight-hundred-acre site (at roughly the same latitude as Jerusalem) where they would live at his feet. No one
knows who threw the first punch. Peace-loving Christians
went to bloody fisticuffs over the Second Coming, with the
whole thing landing in court, in a lawsuit over money that
Rapp loaned to Count Leon early in his stay at Economy.
Rapp called on Etzler to serve as translator during the trial.
Here was proof of their mutual trust and a source of much-
needed cash for Etzler. In a combination of wages and credit,
Rapp advanced Etzler most of $151.[36]

Etzler's next move was to Pittsburgh, where he took a job
as editor of a German-American newspaper, the *Pittsburgher
Beobachter* (Observer). Ten years earlier, an English traveler
described the town as "a poor, gloomy, sickly receptacle,
hardly fit for convicts of the worst description; no greater
punishment could be inflicted . . . upon our bank note forg-
ers than to send them to Pittsburgh." Yet the traveler also

called it a place where "the hammers stunned your ears, and the manufactories struck you dumb with astonishment." Pittsburgh's sickly convicts were actually its white-knuckled entrepreneurs. As much as Pittsburgh stank, Pittsburgh boomed. By the time Etzler arrived, a German community had formed, and the job of editor placed him at the center of things, made him arbiter of the ideas floating around, and positioned him as a public figure. The *Pittsburgh Gazette* announced in June 1833, "A German newspaper called *Der Pittsburgher Beobachter* is issued every Friday by Etzler and Reinhold, No. 74, 3rd Street." Etzler's partner, the otherwise unidentified Reinhold, had stuck with him since Mühlhausen.[37]

•

Yet none of this documents Etzler's inward journey—the one that led him to rectify the idea with the object in his own dialectic. All this time, since the Atlantic passage, he was working through his own idea for a communitarian experiment that would solve the problem of human existence by rescuing people broken by the dislocations of modernity. His settlement would not be predicated on the Second Coming or on any other religious idea. It would not have its member-citizens waiting for deliverance, nor would Etzler ask them to dedicate their possessions and labor for some communal good. He set out to resolve the contradictions between the drudgery, poverty, disease, and sadness he saw on the emaciated faces of backwoods settlers and factory workers and the abundance—the profusion—he observed billowing through the treetops, rising and falling in sea swells, everywhere on Earth.

The world consisted of fruit and force, water and ashes, gravity and sunlight, of beautiful countrysides like the one he had known, where engineers had tamed the River Unstrut. Etzler's *Heimat*, his education in Hegel, and his family history imbued him with a desire to organize social life and create environmental order as an outward sign of the rational idealism he saw operating in the world. Every one of his schemes began with energy. Energy from the sun, wind, and waves would free all people from one of the crucial costs and limitations of production. In 1833 Etzler published *The Paradise Within the Reach of All Men*, the book that he had written during his time in Cincinnati, setting out a world-historical moment:

> Fellow-Men! I promise to show the means for creating a paradise within ten years, where every thing desirable for human life may be had for every man in superabundance, without labor, without pay; where the whole face of nature is changed into the most beautiful form of which it be capable; where man may live in the most magnificent palaces . . . where he may accomplish, without his labor, in one year more than hitherto could be done in thousands of years; he may level mountains, sink valleys, create lakes, drain lakes and swamps, intersect everywhere the land with beautiful canals . . . he may provide himself with means unheard of yet, for increasing his knowledge of the world, and so his intelligence, he may lead a life of continual happiness, of enjoyments unknown.

Philosophy had become worldly, and though the author promised impossible things, something distinguished it from other social experiments. Etzler did not write his treatise on futurity with his eyes closed, but only after looking for years at the United States and the leading lights of the time. One of the oddest thinkers turns out to have been deeply connected to larger currents.

CHAPTER TWO

Paradise Materialized

᳕᳕᳕

E tzler walked the prairie to promote *The Paradise Within the Reach of All Men*, less as an author than as a prophet. He found no disciples among the farmers and townsfolk who paused to listen to this sweaty German who avowed that mirrors could power steam engines. Along the way he sent a letter postmarked Lisbon, Ohio, to Rapp, dated August 26, 1834, asking for payment of one dollar left over from his translating services. But Rapp had died in June, and the new leader of Economy noticed that Etzler owed the entire sum of the line of credit Rapp had extended him— more than one hundred dollars. A Lisbon attorney contacted by Economy found Etzler at the home of a follower from Mühlhausen, preparing to set out for points unknown. The attorney collected the debt on the spot, threatening imprisonment.[1] Etzler quit the prairie and headed south. Cities bloomed as he walked (350 people established a trading post, called Chicago, on the southern shore of Lake Michigan); the sun let off its flares (Hermann von Helmholtz posited a theory of "gravitational contraction" to explain the energy of the sun); and slaves broke their chains (Great Britain abolished the institution), all in 1833–34. Amid the fury of a world popping off with freedom and discovery came a plan for a system of production and social life, without labor, promising the most beautiful surroundings, a kind of wind-powered Schönbrunn Palace for the masses.

Paradise had an architecture. Etzler pictured a manicured landscape, like the lawns and gardens surrounding English country houses, with walks and roads where people would enjoy "the most beautiful scenes imaginable." They would move by canal, gliding "smoothly along between various sceneries of art and nature, in beautiful gondolas" as they took in a view of "fine land and aquatic birds." The inhabitants would live among lavish structures—including walkways covered with porticos, "adorned with magnificent columns, statues and sculptural works . . . while the beauties of nature around heighten the magnificence." There would be wondrous halls, "each two hundred feet square and high," with grand corridors, "each one hundred feet long and twenty wide." There would be eighty galleries, each a thousand feet long, and seven thousand private rooms, "the whole surrounded and intersected by the grandest and most splendid colonnades imaginable . . . all shining, and reflecting to infinity all objects and persons, with splendid lustre of all beautiful colors."

> There will be afforded the most enrapturing views to be fancied, out of the private apartments, from the galleries, from the roof, from its turrets and cupolas—gardens as far as the eye can see, full of fruits and flowers, arranged in the most beautiful order, with walks, colonnades, aqueducts, canals, ponds, plains, amphitheatres, terraces, fountains, sculptural works, pavilions, gondolas, places for public amusement, &c., &c., to delight the eye and fancy, the taste and smell . . . At night the roof, and the

inside and outside of the whole square, are illuminated by gas-light, which in the mazes of many-colored crystal-like colon-nades and vaultings, is reflected with a brilliancy that gives to the whole a lustre of precious stones, as far as the eye can see,— such are the future abodes of men . . . Any member may pro-cure himself all the common articles of his daily wants, by a short turn of some crank, without leaving his apartment. He may, at any time, bathe himself in cold or warm water, or in steam, or in some artificially prepared liquor for invigorating health. He may, at any time, give to the air in his apartment that temperature that suits his feeling best. He may cause, at any time, an agreeable scent of various kinds . . . The crops are gathered and prepared for use without any labor. There is nothing then but enjoyment and delight.

Hot and cold running water, illuminated roofs and walks, agreeable scents, elevators, every convenience, and no work (all by "a short turn of some crank")—it sounds like an Ari-zona retirement village. And that's just the point. Etzler de-signed not a world to come, but the world that came. His knowledge of physics might have been faulty, but his sense that human happiness would be understood as the applica-tion of technology to convenience and leisure was dead-on. And rather than interpret *Paradise* as lunacy, it is more strik-ing to consider all the ways that it reflected the thinking current at the time, the same thinking that has shaped expec-tations for growth into our time. Etzler took a leap, but not a very big one. His machines didn't work, but not because he fancied them as operating on some celestial plane. His great-est fault was his blinding optimism, but in that he was hardly alone.

Etzler was four years old when the French philosopher the Marquis de Condorcet published his *Historical View of the*

Progress of the Human Mind (1795) to prove that "nature has set no term to the perfection of human faculties; that the perfectibility of man is truly indefinite." Progress might vary in its speed, "but it will never be reversed," announced Condorcet.[2] It all sounded good, all that optimism, but how to make it real? By the 1820s, it seemed clear that although humans might be perfectible, all sorts of things prevented them from realizing their potential. They could be enslaved by masters, impoverished by factory owners, and taxed and conscripted by monarchs. Revolution made sense as a clearing of the brush before the new order could be planted, but it lost much of its appeal after the ten-month Reign of Terror orchestrated by Maximilien Robespierre to purify the French Revolution. Robespierre did his clearing with a guillotine and left office by his own execution. Increasingly, intellectuals on the Continent favored small-is-beautiful experiments, making it possible for them to devise social environments and moral economies meant to foster human perfection. Exemplary community suggested a middle way to revolution, since any group of the enlightened who hit upon the right formula would attract others to join them in an ever-widening circle.

The English reformer Robert Owen purchased George Rapp's Second Harmonie settlement, on the Wabash River in Indiana, in 1825, renaming it New Harmony. In 1842 Amos Bronson Alcott and Charles Lane founded Fruitland, near Boston. It compelled the leading American Transcendentalists, including Nathaniel Hawthorne, Ralph Waldo Emerson, and Henry David Thoreau. The Hopedale Community, set up at Milford, Massachusetts, in 1853, represented an experiment in Christian self-sufficiency that included two hundred people in forty-three families. The Icarians declared "a New World . . . of plenty and of equality!" at Nauvoo, Illinois, moving into the town founded by Joseph Smith after the

Mormons abandoned the settlement for the Great Salt Lake in 1847. Shape someone's surroundings and the way they acquire the necessaries of life, they all believed, along with Marx and Feuerbach, and you reshape their morals and outlook. One thinker claimed to have mastered that approach, and he stood out from all the others: Charles Fourier, the French theorist who published *Le Nouveau Monde* in 1829.

Fourier offered a vision of peace and stability, community and harmony through what he called "attractive labor" or "association," in which each person worked as a shareholder, not a wage earner. Said Fourier, "I have discovered the principle and practical mechanism of passional attraction offering to all the nations of the Globe . . . the double charm of pleasurable industry and riches in abundance." When people loved work and trusted one another, they would get rich. For Fourier, nothing divided people and made them poor but the wrongheaded way they governed themselves. His most prominent American interpreter, and the most famous socialist in the United States before the Civil War, was Albert Brisbane of New York. After studying in Paris and Berlin, where he attended Hegel's lectures, Brisbane emerged in the 1840s as an apostle of Fourier, writing at one point, "The evil, misery and injustice, now predominant on the earth, have not their foundation in political or administrative errors," nor in a depraved human nature, "but in the FALSE ORGANIZATION OF SOCIETY ALONE."[3]

Fourier's far-reaching influence came from his plausible design for living—the phalanx, a village consisting of fifteen hundred people. Nineteenth-century American intellectuals seized the form as Society 2.0. George and Sophia Ripley transformed a dairy farm near Roxbury, Massachusetts, into an idealist community, calling it the Brook Farm Phalanx. There was an Ohio Phalanx, a Sangamon Phalanx in Illinois,

more than one in Pennsylvania, and a North American Phalanx consisting of 673 acres in Monmouth County, New Jersey, founded by Brisbane, with Horace Greeley, editor of the
New York Tribune, as vice president.[4] Etzler's belief in exemplary community as a way of eliminating competition and resolving the contradictions of modernity came right out of
Fourier, and the reason is plain. Fourier showed everyone
how it could be done, even sketching the buildings and by-
laws guaranteed to make every phalanx a success. Under all
the philosophy, all the verbosity, Fourier's thinking caught on
in the United States because it had a hammer-and-nail sim-
plicity. Build it, and they will live in peace. And yet, a phalanx
was only a modestly self-sufficient town. Fourier had in mind
a happy kind of work; Etzler sought to eliminate work altogether and to unveil an economic regime so compelling that
Congress and President Andrew Jackson would promote it.
Etzler wanted to erase the boundary between a phalanx and
the rest of society, to open its gates and flood the world.[5]

Progress came to consist of harder stuff than the reveries
of utopians. It could be measured statistically as advances in
mill production, canal transportation, and farm productivity.
But stark materialism and socialist idealism did not sit on either side of an ideological divide. Etzler's statement—"The
world is yet large enough to afford superabundance of all
necessaries and comforts of human life, for many ages to
come, for the whole humankind"—could have come from almost any of the significant political economists of the 1830s.[6]
Behind every economic scheme lay an assumption so powerful that it transcended political difference, uniting utilitarian
capitalists and Hegelian socialists: God had created everything living and inert to serve as feed and fuel for human advancement. By the nineteenth century, that belief had settled
in so deeply that it marked the way people thought about so-

ciety itself. Some ceased to describe civilization as a contract or as the rule of law, the way liberal thinkers had in the past, instead depicting it as a perpetual process of wealth creation and market activity aided and accelerated by invention. The infinite love of God had been replaced by the infinite powers and resources of the earth.

In 1834 Etzler set out to test his theories, build his palaces, and gather followers. For a time, we've lost his path. Following him now means opening his ideas as if they were packages—to see what lies inside them.

•

The basis of my proposal is, that there are powers in nature at the disposal of man, a million times greater than all men on earth could effect, with their united exertions, by their nerves and sinews . . . They are derived . . . from the motions of the atmosphere, from sun-shine, and from the motions of the sea, caused by the gravity of the moon or by wind . . . The question is not, whether the stated powers may be somewhat less or more than stated, but whether they are of such a gigantic magnitude as to afford a sufficiency for all our wants. —*J. A. Etzler*[7]

In the 1830s everything seemed to burn with a newly contained fire, but at a time when almost every other inventor and economic theorist imagined a world glowing with coal, Etzler turned away from any earthen substance for providing energy, even for heat-producing engines. Instead, he attempted to harness the quotidian energy that wraps itself around us all the time—the breeze at the shore, the fall of a playground swing. These needed only mechanical expression to provide all the energy humankind would ever require. The mystique of Etzler to those who followed him in the 1840s radiated from his draftsmanlike confidence that he knew of ways to give mechanical form to powers obvious but elusive. The forces he favored had no biological or geological substance, could not be squandered or sold, could never run dry or burden people under their oppressive cost—"mighty powers in nature that neither eat, nor drink, nor sleep, nor perish."[8] With wind, tides, and sunlight, "no material is consumed." Imagine windmills two hundred feet high and spaced evenly over one square mile. Etzler said that such an array would generate 10,000 horsepower, equal to the bodily exertion of 100,000 people. But the winds never slept, so he doubled the number, saying that windmills did the work of double the people in a twenty-four-hour period. He dreamed of sails spaced all over the earth—more than two hundred million square miles of land and sea! Added up, the power generated would equal the muscle of forty trillion people.[9] Said the author, "The requisite stuffs for rendering this power . . . are co-extensive with the whole world."

Beginning in the nineteenth century, progress became almost synonymous with energy-intensive production—the making of more things with more concentrated force. It is not the engine that does the work, after all, but the combustion of fuel that overcomes resistance to friction and gravity. When we think about manufacturing, we tend to think of the *matter* transformed, but while matter can run scarce, it is by far the more abundant factor. Production is equally an expression of *energy*, but what is energy? The physicist Richard Feynman told students in one lecture, "It is important to realize that in physics today, we have no knowledge of what energy *is* . . . It is an abstract thing." It can be measured, but we know it only by what it does. Energy is the capacity to do work, and work is the transfer of energy from body A to body B.[10] Energy is everywhere and nowhere. A million stars burn in the night sky, but the heat and light available on

Earth from the nearest star is surprisingly meager—between 125 and 237 watts per square meter (W/m²) per year are received at the surface. Only a tiny fraction of this amount exists at any given time in plants and animals, and solar energy accumulates in only one durable form—petroleum. Energy is scarce, and concentrated energy is even scarcer.[11]

Etzler's obsession with energy came from the insight that it virtually determined the social conditions of labor. For all of human history before the eighteenth century, power for work came from the sun, and the only way to harvest it was by eating. But growing food required land—the basis of class in agrarian societies. When elites mediated the flow of energy through the control of land, they transformed energy into a social relation. Lords and peasants participated in a coerced energy exchange in which the latter handed over food under threat of violence from the former, who lived by confiscating meat and wheat on a scale that ranged from village to kingdom to empire. Accumulating vast amounts of energy meant accumulating vast numbers of bodies, a fact that changes the way we understand such imperial projects as the Pyramids and the Great Wall of China. Etzler called industrialism a vicious energy monopoly. Nothing but the *cost* of coal dictated that the Many would sweat for wages in factories owned by the Few. If he could destroy this monopoly by making coal valueless, he would change everything. People would live where they wanted and produce what they wanted, regardless of their capital. Everyone would live like royalty because the command of resources and the ability to consume that defined the rich would belong to everyone.

Etzler had good reason to believe that energy on a revolutionary scale would soon be available. The boldest, most imaginative physical theorist of the time said as much in a short treatise that Etzler would have read during his education as an engineer. In 1824 Nicolas-Léonard-Sadi Carnot, a French mathematician, published *Reflections on the Motive Power of Heat*, which first described the way heat passed from hot to cold bodies, resulting in its capacity to perform work. Carnot unified the forces of the heavens and the earth, showing all energy to be heat from the sun. "It causes the agitations of the atmosphere, the ascension of clouds, the fall of rain and of meteors, the currents of water which channel the surface of the globe." The sun brought into being plants and other "combustibles," providing people with "the power to produce, at all times and in all places, heat and the impelling power which is the result of it." Carnot called the sun an "immense reservoir" from which humans "may draw the moving force necessary for our purposes."[12] These insights, however, could be misleading. The sun alone does not form combustibles, but Etzler, along with some significant scientists, seized upon the idea that physical forces created life. He not only claimed to have harnessed infinite energy, but also to have circumvented the scarcity of energy in its material forms.

Engineers and scientific thinkers throughout Europe and the United States thought the same way. Consider Thomas Ewbank, an inventor who stood for all the besotted optimism that thinking about coal sometimes aroused. Ewbank was an English-born scientist who manufactured metal tubing in New York before serving as the United States commissioner of patents. He may be best known for his accounts of life and customs in Brazil, published in the 1850s. As an industrial philosopher, he clung tightly to an idealization of physical nature, linking the supply of natural resources to human potential and divine intention. "Who can inform us where the terminus is to be?" he asked. "No one; for there is nothing in ourselves, nor in the earth's resources, to point out where the

last step is to land us . . . It is a rational belief that there are
no limits to [man's] advancement, as there appear to be none
to the agents of it nor to his power over them." Coal got him
even more excited: "A first element of progress for all time, it
is preposterous to suppose the supplies of coal can ever be exhausted or even become scarce." Preposterous, he said, because it formed continually in "the depths of our oceans,"
faster than people could burn it. Ewbank even maintained
that coal furnished energy in *unlimited* quantities: "The
proposition is, that unlimited amounts of force are to be
drawn out of inert matter."[13]

Yet Carnot's physics, unlike Ewbank's, possessed a profound economy. He noted that heat balances out—no losses,
no gains—as it is released and then captured to perform mo-
mentary work. Further investigation along these lines resulted in the second law of thermodynamics—the most
important physical principle to be discovered in the nineteenth century. Energy is not recyclable. Its transfer causes it
to dissipate, and it can never be recaptured. The energy is not
gone, but it becomes unavailable to heat anything, move anything, make anything. All this relates directly to matter because energy is not disembodied—it always takes physical
form (even in the sun), so its release causes the dissipation
of matter as well. This is entropy: the irreversible transition
from wood to ashes. Ewbank needed to kill the theory, which
was then being scrutinized and tested by scientists, in order
for the world as he imagined it to make sense. He proposed
"millions of dollars in experiments" to prove "that heat can
be used as a motive agent over and over again: in other
words, that power can repeat itself."[14] The implications could
not have been starker. If power could not repeat itself, then
the depletion of coal became a possibility. (A more reflective
mind struggled with the same problem. In 1851 William

Thomson, known as Lord Kelvin, wrote privately, "Everything in the material world is progressive." He meant that things always moved in one direction, never "back to any previous state." During an extraordinary period of discovery and gestation, Thomson finally accepted entropy: "I believe that no physical action can ever restore the heat emitted from the sun, and that this source is not inexhaustible.")[15]

Carnot's thinking about the sun also ricocheted around the scientific world in that bright morning before almost anyone fully understood the second law of thermodynamics. He said that the sun produced combustibles, giving humans easy sources of energy at all times and in all places. Research into plants seemed to reveal that wind and sunlight—not biological systems—caused them to grow, and wind and sunlight appeared to have no limit. The German chemist Justus von Liebig reported that carbon—the essential element within all forms of life—came from the atmosphere, not the soil. The discovery of the carbon cycle stands as one of the greatest achievements of organic chemistry, but Liebig went too far with it. He claimed, wildly, "The amount of materials contained in the atmosphere, suited to the nourishment of plants . . . must be abundantly sufficient to cover the whole surface of the earth with a rich vegetation . . . All that plants require for their development is conveyed to them by the incessant motions of the atmosphere."[16] Liebig denied the nutritional role of humus, the layer of decaying plants and microbes covering many types of topsoil. Humus looked to him like a meaningless mishmash because he had no way of analyzing its many components (including the role of microorganisms in the carbon cycle), so he constructed a theory built entirely from what he did know—that a key nutrient came from the air.

The sun looked more promising as a source of earthly abundance. John William Draper was a chemist best known for taking the first photograph of the moon, in 1840. In 1844 he observed that plants grew only where the sun reached them, so he deduced that sunlight caused their genesis—their "organization." Draper appeared to ignore soil—the environment, in other words—as having any role in plant development. Zachariah Allen, a manufacturer and engineer, spent years thinking about steam engines, concluding that organic and physical nature could be understood as manifestations of the same "electric matter" originating in the sun. "The action of the sun," Allen wrote, "transforms atoms of carbon into mineral coal and wood, serving as fuel, and into fruits, grasses, and grains, serving as food."[17] Etzler thought the same way—vegetation needed only "solar heat, light, and water," nothing whatsoever from the living earth.[18]

All these scientists had Liebig's problem: they had great difficulty reading any systematic law into green and wriggling stuff other than the confounded life cycle. Life told them things they did not want to hear—that expansion in any system balanced out as a cost somewhere else. They much preferred to interpret life as mechanical, caused by wind pushing carbon atoms around or sunlight creating plants. These forces characterized the entire universe, not just the muddy Earth, and since they never ran out, they suggested that life could be endlessly generated.

The scientists did not have it wrong, but they had only part of the picture. Science assembles models of reality in pieces. No one understood the delicate energetics of ecosystems until the twentieth century. Nonetheless, a vision of the human economy running parallel with physical laws took shape during this time of rapid discovery. Economic thinkers took what accorded with their views and then stopped listening. Science moved on, in other words, but most of the social theorists never did. The troubling thing is that economic growth still has nineteenth-century physics as its intellectual touchstone.

•

All things desirable for human life, when once known, may be rapidly multiplied, without labour or expense, to superabundance for everyone; and wealth becomes as cheap as water.
                                                                    —*J. A. Etzler*

Economy, from the Greek, originally meant "the management of households," and political economists more or less agreed that the careful and prudent management of limited quantities prevented waste and debt. But they applied a different standard to states. If they acknowledged scarcity at all, they insisted that it could be only a relative, not an absolute, condition. This denial of even the possibility of scarcity did not come from a few thinkers—it was nearly universal. Political economy is not economics, a more recent study that uses mathematical language to arrive at highly focused conclusions, such as why firms behave as they do in times of recession, or the consequences of a government's currency policy. Political economy concerns the material constitution of societies—how they organize labor and production, how they regulate trade and define the role of government, and where wealth comes from. Amid the turbulence of the eighteenth and nineteenth centuries, political economy became the primary way that social thinkers described, interpreted, and argued about progress.

Everything seemed to be changing so fast, especially the money being made and the products being turned out. Cities expanding, a working class forming, the astonishing onset of the market as the overarching institution—someone needed to explain these things in a way that emphasized their continuity with the past. The theory of stages served the purpose well by depicting progress as the outcome of human nature acting against the environment over long periods, and the same theory justified civil society as the urban/bureau-cratic/commercial plateau of history by cutting off any possibility of future evolution. In this epoch-making moment, different historical rules took over. Henceforth modern institutions would *expand*. Change took the form of greater production, larger markets, fresh territory, and rising population. New lands and new peoples would be absorbed, spreading security from want to people who still languished in a savage state. The most important thing to know about this first model of economic growth is that expansion *solved all problems and created none*. Though writers differed in all sorts of ways (such as whether governments should protect domestic manufacturing with tariffs or adopt free-trade policies), all who believed in progress agreed that the achievement of modernity equaled a condition of never-ending growth.

The need for raw material to supply expansion was so obvious that there wasn't much to say about it. Jacob Cardozo of Charleston, South Carolina, launched his *Notes on Political Economy* (1826) with this omnibus statement: "No system of wealth can be complete . . . which does not ascribe equal effect to the powers and principles of the material world in raising, manufacturing and transporting those products to which value is annexed."[19] Victor Riqueti, Marquis de Mirabeau, said a little more. Mirabeau tried to build a model of the French state from its basis in agricultural production, so he connected land and politics with an intensity unequaled by any of his contemporaries. In order to understand politics at all, he wrote in 1763, "we must consider the common weal in terms of its essence, and humanity as a whole in terms of its root, *subsistence*." But subsistence required work. Of the three factors of production, labor stood apart from land and capital as the bodily form of the energy needed to turn field into food, cattle into beef, first nature into second. The most elegant formulation came from Karl Marx, who defined labor as "a process by which man, through his own actions, mediates, regulates and controls the metabolism between himself and nature."[20]

No one knew the extent of environmental capacity, so none had any way of measuring it against the force of labor. Political economists treated labor as variable and nature as constant. "As human wants increase, in the progress of man from his primitive state towards that of civilization," stated one American, "so must his labor for their supply." Simple as that. Labor made all good things happen: it improved land, advanced the practical arts, and stepped up production. Charles Babbage, the English mechanical engineer who invented the difference engine—often considered the first computer—took it to the extreme: "The cost of any article may be reduced in its ultimate analysis to the quantity of *labour* by which it was procured."[21] Adam Smith noticed that more people ate more fish, causing shortfalls. No problem, just add labor. "The fish must generally be sought for at a greater distance, larger vessels must be employed, and more expensive machinery of every kind made use of. The real price of this commodity, therefore, naturally rises in the progress of improvement." The additional labor and material needed to pull in the catch drives up the price, but that's all for the best because when people pay more, they add to the gross product of the state. This is the Enlightenment alchemy that transformed consumption into wealth.[22]

Economy internalized its own rules without checking to see if they accorded with the way nature functioned. Fueling the craziness was what can only be described as the economic equivalent of Providence, or the care and sustenance given by God. Nothing else explains why the people who thought most about the economy failed to acknowledge its effects. A writer for the *Southern Quarterly Review* tried to explore the question. "How then is the quantity [of any commodity] kept good," he asked, "since a great encroachment is made upon it by the expenditure of every day?" Don't worry, he answered, for "the strength and skill of the human hand . . . assisted by the mechanical and productive energies of the material world, are always equal to the supply of human wants." A follower of Fourier put it this way: "The unity of man with nature implies, that men . . . shall obtain such control or mastery of the natural elements, that nature . . . shall fully minister to human advancement." The American political economist Amasa Walker argued in 1866 that wealth is "a perpetual progress, an unceasing self-multiplication." People's wants are not a debit but a credit; they are "the springs of wealth."[23] There would always be enough, they all said, because nothing made sense any other way. Providence, in its secular form, supported a big theory on an imaginary foundation.

A century before *The Wealth of Nations*, one of the earliest economic thinkers imagined infinite supplies for infinite wants. In 1690 Nicholas Barbon, a London merchant and member of the East India Company, wrote a tract arguing for a policy of vigorous trade. He somehow believed that the "native staple" of any country "is perpetual, and never to be consumed." Beasts, fowls, and fishes naturally increase, and "the minerals of the earth are unexhaustable." He then reasoned, "If the natural stock be infinite, the artificial stock that is made of the natural, must be infinite." But won't a fortune waste away when spending exceeds income? "This is true, of a person, but not of a nation; because his estate is finite, but the stock of a nation infinite." Conservation made no sense to him because "what is infinite can neither receive addition by parsimony, nor suffer diminution by prodigality."[24] Barbon pursued a point. He wanted to demolish mercantilism, a commercial strategy of hoarding gold that conceived of all money as strictly limited. Barbon said that it's not the gold itself that creates wealth, but its circulation—what we might call the value added from trade. Since exchange would go on forever, so would accumulation. But here's the point: Barbon needed fowls and fish to be infinite in order for the model to work, because behind circulation, real people consumed real things; if these ran short, then the mercantilists would have been right.

One spoiler wasn't lulled by promises of infinity. Like an anvil smashing a wedding cake came Thomas Robert Malthus into the celebration of plenty. Originator of the most famous argument against progress, *An Essay on the Principle of Population* (1798), Malthus turned Enlightenment optimism on its head. As the dismal parson saw it, a population reproducing geometrically (by factors: 2, 4, 8, 16) would eventually overtake a food supply increasing arithmetically (by units: 1, 2, 3, 4). Malthus dropped the red velvet curtain on the pageant of plenty. "I see no way," he wrote, "by which man can escape from the weight of this law which pervades all animated nature." No law or policy could slow its inexorable unfolding, "even for a single century." Though lacking any evidence, his arguments seemed just plausible enough to cause a panic in the intellectual world. Malthus revealed, to the horror of his readers, that the inhabitants of civil society never had and never would escape the scramble for food. In the long run, they could not count on living in "ease, happiness, and comparative leisure," free from anxiety about providing the means of subsistence for their families.[25] Every advance brought humanity that much closer to destruction. The abundance flowing from land only encouraged the excess population that would, before long, come charging into the storehouse of humanity like a plague. In his only lasting contribution to economic thought, Malthus hit upon the law of diminishing returns, or the idea that at a certain point, increasing units of labor result in less and less additional output.

The *Essay* provoked fifty years of furious, raging argument by critics who attacked its author's assumptions and presented every imaginable exception.[26] William Godwin, whose writing first sparked Malthus, spoke for the majority when he asserted that surplus had created civil society in the first place: "The basis of civil society . . . will be found in the truth of this proposition, that man in society is capable of rearing a greater quantity of provisions than is necessary for his own subsistence." Others claimed that Malthus neglected the power of trade to counteract scarcity. Civilized people don't eat from within rural townships; they trade over oceans, using markets to distribute the productions of the earth. Nor do they accept whatever the uncultured countryside issues them. British critics pointed out how their countrymen drained marshes to eliminate wasteland, mixed manure into soils to increase yields, rotated crops, improved cattle by breeding, and generally coaxed a greater bounty than Malthus, apparently, imagined (though it was going on right under his nose). Friedrich Engels was one of the few who attacked Malthus for his cruelty and for the God-driven determinism that made misery contingent on Christian virtue. Malthus blamed the poor, dismissing them to starvation and death, without so much as a word of criticism for the rich—the greater consumers. Engels called the *Essay* vile, hideous, "the crudest, most barbarous theory that ever existed, a system of despair." When environmentalists of the 1970s embraced Malthus, they did so by ignoring the entire social and religious thrust of the *Essay*.[27]

In the daybreak of a new energy economy, when greasy rocks held a billion infernos, who took seriously tales of scarcity? Even if it were true that population always pressed against the means of production, a crisis seemed impossibly distant. For most Americans, the earth looked vacant, not full. The British-born chemist and economist Thomas Cooper observed in 1831, "Hardly one half of the cultivatable regions of the earth, are settled . . . Nor is the economy of food perfectly understood as yet. Man is but a recent inhabitant of the earth; and we live in the infancy of improvement."[28] Others argued against Malthus by insisting that land restored itself. "It is impossible to conjecture a limit to the increase of population," wrote the American political economist Erasmus Peshine Smith, "if man will but conform to the law which Nature exemplifies in all her processes, by which the soil regains whatever material of nutriment it has lent for the support of vegetable and animal life."[29] All these believers in the harmony of man and nature shared Etzler's faith that there could be greater stability in human subsistence than previous generations had known. "My system proves," wrote Etzler, "how this miserable scramble and universal poverty and suffering may be made to cease forever."

When Etzler insisted on untapped energy leading to wealth as a generalized condition, possible for all people living and unborn, he spoke a language at once idealist and materialist, theoretical and practical, well within the dialogue of physics and political economy. The universe seemed to be ready to reveal some great secret, and he shared that dizzying faith with scientists as well as socialists.[30] With all this in mind, he sought land that could be organized and molded

into a vision of beauty. For if he had learned anything from
the Prussians, it was that land reflected the desires of the people who had power over it. He moved to install that power
with a mechanical footprint and let it walk across the earth.

•

*Suppose extensive tracts of land, cleared at once from their sponta-
neous growth, . . . the rivers and creeks confined in properly nar-
rowed channels by dams, the swamps drained by ditches, or filled
up . . . suppose such an improvement to be, not for some hundreds
of acres as you find them now at most, but for 10, 20, or more
miles in diameter—and you will have a climate as fine and
healthy as anywhere on the globe may be found . . . Your hideous
wilderness, that is now but the habitation of brutes and venomous
or loathsome vermin and a few scattered miserable Indians, will
rapidly become the delightful abodes of happy intelligent human
beings. By a simple application of the new means, the soil, so prepared, will be covered with luxuriant growth of all desirable veg-
etables that the climate admits of, the finest gardens extending
many miles in every direction, in beautiful arrangement and
symmetry, will at once appear. Snakes, mosketoes, and other trou-
blesome vermin will have disappeared, the causes of their existence
being annihilated!*   —*J. A. Etzler*

Every land system is a social system. Human communities
spell out their tightly held principles in fields and boundaries.
Think of Soviet collectivization, English enclosure, or the
American homestead. Families, governments, and economies
exist in space—fundamentally, in agrarian space. Ever since
people began to emphasize planting and herding over hunting and gathering, they have created exclusive spaces in order
to keep their wheat and cattle safe from wildlife that would
breed with them, trample them, or carry them off in the

night. Farmers drew sharp distinctions between inside and outside. House, field, country, state—these became totalizing visions, where wildlife needed segregation if not annihilation. Utopia has often reflected the same totalizing vision by admitting of nothing from the imperfect world beyond its borders, and utopians have often sought to eradicate before inventing.[31] Albert Brisbane, the American follower of Fourier, believed that "the *terrestrial* Destiny of man is to OVERSEE the globe," and he called for "a general and perfect cultivation of its surface," including deserts planted, swamps drained, and forests harvested.[32] Only then would a liberated people see their reflection in the landscape.

Etzler could have established a factory village, but that form would have been difficult to reproduce and would have tied him to suppliers and banks and other real-world institutions. He sought something entire, unlike anything attempted before, which suggested a space he could wipe clean. Just as the federal survey extended its sections and townships in every direction, Etzler meant to replicate his orbits, circuits, and dominions beyond political borders. "The association," he said, "is limited to no particular country or place, or number of members, and may extend to any part of the world, by co-ordinate branches . . . Thus you may spread a net over the whole world, not for ensnaring, oppressing, and enslaving men as has been done hitherto, but for exercising the most beneficial influence." When it came to territory, universal brotherhood dressed in imperial uniform. Call it Etzler's Prussian peace with nature. Land had to be won militarily, organized socially, occupied technologically, and made profitable economically before settlers could sing Schiller's "Ode to Joy" with their eyes raised. Creating a symbolic landscape always means declaring war.[33]

Land is the oldest form of expansion, representing—at

once—the most fundamental compulsions of agrarian societies and the furthering of economic growth as it later emerged. One of the first stories ever recorded, Joshua's incursion across the Jordan River with an army of thirty thousand Israelites, describes a genocidal war of territorial annexation. Impelled by a land use that tends to diminish returns from soil, agrarian people have sought continually to accumulate their primary resource. In the nineteenth century, the great gambits for power and political design began with the use and control of land. The blood and thunder of state formation in North America had many parts—railroad construction, rocketing cotton production, accelerating factory output—but it fell hardest in the form of ferocious violence against Indians. Andrew Jackson signed the Indian Removal Act of 1830, legalizing the forced eviction of seventeen thousand Cherokee, sending them on a fatal overland journey so that he could open their land to white farmers. The Sac and Fox moved to reclaim their homeland in Illinois, bringing on hideous white retaliation in the Black Hawk War of 1832. The Second Seminole War, a relentless seven-year campaign to subdue Florida, ended in 1842. At the same time, southern planters led by Stephen Austin and Sam Houston, who had settled under Mexican authority in the northern province of Tejas, instigated a war for independence in 1835, declaring the Republic of Texas the following year. Expansion can't be boiled down to any one motive. It was deeply political, infused with ethnic fears and hatreds, and impossible to extricate from the failing balance of power in Congress over slavery. Sectional struggle took the ancient form, however, in an attempt to relieve mounting conflict through a blatantly biophysical enlargement of the productive resources of the state.

It is no accident that the most vigorous American debate

on Malthus and his Principle of Population took place before and during the war with Mexico, when President James K. Polk, urged on by expansionists, ordered the invasion of Mexico without provocation. The most explicit reference came from Lewis Cass of Michigan, secretary of war under Andrew Jackson and a member of Congress at the time. Cass saw teeming multitudes pent up in the cities, threatening the social order: "In Europe, one of the social evils is concentration . . . There is not room for expansion . . . We want almost unlimited power of expansion. That is our safety valve." Cass projected that the United States would one day be as populous as the empire of China. The most significant geographer in the United States, William Darby, justified war as the solution to the problem of scarce real estate. Americans would consume themselves out of existence without more land, he said. In answer to a query put to him by John C. Calhoun, Darby foretold a population of 23 million by 1850 and 102.8 million by 1900. Polk himself appealed directly to Malthus as grounds for war: "Upon the breaking out of the war of the revolution, our numbers scarcely equaled 3,000,000 of souls; they already exceed 17,000,000, and will continue to progress in a ratio which duplicates in a period of about 23 years." Polk had his eye on a piece of earth extending from the base of the Rocky Mountains to the mouth of the Columbia River, about 770 million acres.[34]

There was no Malthusian crisis in the South or anywhere else—only stagnation in the employment of slave labor and planter capital as existing methods of production ran up against environmental constraints to growth. Planters needed more land in order to reproduce their entire social and material existence. Liberals, going back to John Locke, made almost no distinction between the possession of land and the establishment of democracy. Thomas Jefferson, in particular, understood that the rights and equality promised in the founding documents of the United States would never have entered the lived experience of its people were it not for the soils, game, and timber that made every white settler the equal of every other, providing each an endowment that made him independent of wealthy proprietors. Members of Congress from the South and West repeatedly acknowledged this fact by voting for generous land laws as a way of diffusing population, and thus political power, over as great a territory as possible. The survey system itself created a tableau that subdivided the public domain down to the capillary level, a kind of federal structure on the map—state, county, township, and section. The imperative to replicate American institutions and material life coincided with the imperative of capital. Underdeveloped regions act as magnets for capital because they offer spectacular returns and keep capital fully employed, staving off sluggish production and low returns. For all these reasons, the Mexican War looked like a giant welfare policy, one that would serve labor as well as capital, communitarian socialist as well as free-market capitalist. Both sought new spaces they could control in order to maintain one or another model of the common good.[35]

Socialist reformers shadowed the manic aggrandizement of the Polk administration. Brigham Young sent a volunteer company of Mormons to link up with General Stephen Kearny as Kearny marched toward California. They had orders to scout out possible sites for a settlement. In 1847 Young founded Salt Lake City in what became the Territory of Utah. Urban artisans also had their eye on Mexican land. Etzler's faith in democratic settlement had its most proximate context in a radical political movement founded by George Henry Evans, a newspaper editor from New York City. Evans established the National Reform Association (NRA) in 1844 with a membership taken mostly from the trade unions. The members lobbied Congress and ran their own candidates to secure homestead legislation, worked to exempt farmland from seizure in the collection of debts, and even tried to thwart large estates by law. In 1845 Albert Brisbane endorsed land reform, throwing the nation's Fourierists into the fight for the NRA's legislative goals.[36] Etzler incorporated the NRA's most visible plank into his own system when he called on the United States to issue homesteads in order to "rapidly draw a vast concourse of emigrants from the older parts of the United States, and chiefly from Europe, to our unsettled western country."[37]

In its many variations, land reform inspired millions of working people on both sides of the Atlantic to seek a better existence. Jamie L. Bronstein concludes that reformers felt "bound by the common notions that the right to life entailed the right to the wherewithal to live, that society bore a responsibility for the physical welfare and social happiness of its citizens." Behind the idealism, however, land reform had its own war policy. Its supporters might have believed differently, but by seeking social solutions in Indian country, they expressed the same commitment to Manifest Destiny as Polk himself. This is the context for Etzler's call for the annihilation of Indians. Etzler revealed that he understood the human cost of land reform but that the blessed ends justified the bloody means. He sounded just like Thomas Ewbank (in many ways Etzler's industrialist counterpart), who also believed that human destiny depended on land seized from savages. Writing as commissioner of patents, he submitted what must be the most disturbing report of any government official. " 'Onward!' is the standing order of God," he shrieked. "Those who refuse to obey must be pushed aside—such is the inflexible fiat of Heaven." The weakhearted could not see how "the disinheriting and consequent annihilation of the entire occupants of half the globe can accord with Divine justice . . . they cannot see—simply because they have yet to learn that the Creator has ordained distinct and independent laws for the material as for the moral world."[38] Communitarian socialists, including Horace Greeley and Brigham Young, sympathized with Indians, but the fact remains that American-style utopia depended on midnight massacres and broken treaties. The irony of land reform is that while it set out to free people from the slow death of slums and shop floors, it reproduced some of the same patterns of the civilization it rejected.

Etzler shared the mission of National Reform, but he floated above politics, never coming down to slug it out at party conventions or among members of Congress. He gave the same answer to every political question—abundance trumped the need for compromise. The land system centered on the Satellite would eventually take over every continent, doing away with poverty, aristocratic privilege, and class in an end run around the actual. Without a moment's reflection, he transferred the same logic that failed in North America to England and then to Venezuela under the assumption that science cuts across all distinctions. Here, too, Etzler mirrored the deep assumptions of those who would advocate economic growth as a social program, since they also believed that the constant creation of wealth, made possible by energy and machinery, neutralized the politics of class. Like neoliberals today, Etzler blithely ignored his failures and the collateral damage of expansion itself as in no way related to the principles he followed.

With the motives came the tools. At the same time that Etzler conceived of the Satellite, other engineers experimented with their own designs for occupying as much land as possible with as little labor as possible. Cyrus Hall Mc-Cormick first tested his reaping machine in Rockbridge

County, Virginia, in 1831. Obed Hussey came up with one very similar in 1833. But the only machine to approach the Satellite in its multifunctioned, clank-and-clatter brilliance was Hiram Moore's combined harvester and thresher, first tested in Kalamazoo County, Michigan, in 1831. Blades cut the wheat, feeding it to a cylinder that lifted it up and over, dropping it onto a vibrating screen that separated the kernels from the straw and chaff. A fan blew the chaff away as the kernels fell into burlap sacks. (Too cumbersome and expensive for the average farmer—it needed sixteen horses to pull it—the first combine flopped, to be invented again years later in California.) The reaper and the combine held out the big dream: that energy and mechanics would free people from labor, delivering more food and greater stability to their lives. They were growth machines in that very simple sense—they swelled the size of the economy by accelerating the transfer of resources into commodities. Anyone would sympathize with that goal, since one of its results was a larger, healthier society. Pulling the focus back, however, might change the way we look at growth. Civil society depended on expansion to continually prove and maintain itself, yet expansion boxed it in by pinning human progress to biophysical growth—a phenomenon with inherent limits, requiring violence and finally imperialism.

•

Americans! It is now in your power, to become within 10 years a nation to rule the world. Your territory can contain, in all affluence imaginable, from 200 to 300 millions of human individuals, as many as the Chinese empire contains now.   —J. A. Etzler

Population: no other measure of progress so fascinated materialist thinkers, some of whom placed an increasing humanity at the center of their theories of wealth. Deep in the brain stem of agrarian society lies the idea that humans are a form of natural capital. For thousands of years and into the industrial era, material progress meant human increase. The reasoning was simple: Each additional person added a unit to the amount of labor-power in a society. More people harvested more, built more, and cleared more land. Until very recently, before the steam engine magnified labor to attain unprecedented efficiencies, no other form of growth existed. An English critic of Malthus, George Ensor, wrote, "Men are merchandise, without referring to the slave trade. They are money, without being stamped at the mint. Many men are themselves a great machine."[39] A common formulation said that population created the means of its own subsistence. Another anti-Malthusian turned the tables on consumption: "The increase of population is so far from having any tendency to overstock, that the more rapid and extensive it is, it necessarily supplies human wants more completely, augments more largely the average amount of employment, income, and wealth, renders civilization more complete."[40] No one actually argued that too few people, not too many, caused famine, but many political economists blithely asserted that many, when skillfully employed, created their own means of subsistence.

As President Polk observed, the population of the United States hit 17 million in 1840, an increase of 4.2 million from the census of 1830 and of 7 million from 1820. The staggering rise made people ask an unprecedented question: How many could the world hold? The subject transcended Malthus and his *Essay*. Scores of writers sensed something big coming, like a whale surfacing. The growth curve of world population remained nearly flat for six thousand years, up to about 3000 B.C. (about five thousand years before the present), when it began a slow rise. Then, within just a few decades, it took a nearly vertical turn, passing the one billion mark sometime between 1800 and 1810. Etzler knew of the one billion figure, and it inspired him to present his own tally of a future humanity. He noted that the surface of the globe consists of about two hundred million square miles, of which half (he estimated) was free of winter. He proposed that one acre in the temperate or tropical zones would feed sixteen people—one square mile would feed close to ten thousand. He did the math. One hundred million square miles would sustain one trillion people. It required a truly strange imagination to predict that the earth could sustain one thousand times its present population—and to promote that as a sign of progress.

Something fundamental had changed that made Etzler think that the world could sustain one trillion people. Agriculture had shattered its own ceiling. The rising availability of food in Europe seems like a minor story next to industrialism, but that first expansion made the second one possible. At the beginning of the eighteenth century, the energy supply in a typical French diet (roughly 1,850 calories a day) equaled that of Rwanda in 1965, the year the World Bank named it the most malnourished nation in the world. Robert Fogel points out that at that level of nutrition, even the strongest males have limited vigor for work. Work energy is residual, meaning that it consists of the calories left over after metabolism. In the United States circa 2007, an adult male had 2,600 calories available for work; in 1807, an English worker had 858. Go back to the 1770s in Germany, just twenty years before Etzler was born, and harvests recurrently failed, causing starvation in Saxony and Prussia. No wonder eighteenth-century economists upheld agriculture as the basis of all wealth! Trade and manufacturing might earn money, but what kind of society do you have when nobody but the aristocracy has enough oomph to do more than get up in the morning? The taxable wealth of early-modern agriculture can be understood as calories over and above basic metabolism—a net product that made other forms of production viable. Progress, in one sense, denoted the capacity of a nation to sustain a growing number of people.[41]

For all the hullabaloo about coal and waterpower, food remained the most crucial source of energy. Fogel argues that people became larger and more energetic beginning around 1900, but some of that change hit half a century earlier. A revolution that began on the island of Great Britain spread to the United States in the 1820s, radically accelerating the productivity of land and its capacity to endure cropping year after year without decline. Cattle manure, wetland drainage, and convertible husbandry that rotated fields and pasture—these ended famine in Britain by 1624, and their cumulative impact caused a sharp increase in the population of the island throughout the eighteenth century. By 1820 England saw its humans increase by 1.5 percent a year, an amazing reversal in less than two centuries. The population of the American colonies (and then the United States) doubled every twenty-three years beginning in the early seventeenth century, with an abundance of food energy that fueled fertility rates while mortality declined. European cities depended on in-migration from the higher birthrates of the countryside until the 1840s, when cities finally began to generate their own populations.[42] These are some of the changes Etzler might have noticed. So while the big boost that Fogel documents had not yet begun, population already reflected a stability unknown in Europe before.

The pieces begin to shape a formula. Energy in the form of sun, wind, and waves—inexhaustible and detached from any biological form—plus the presumed inexhaustibility of soils and forests and all resources, plus magnificent machines to render the forces of the earth economically visible, would turn out calories to sustain a population of one trillion people, resolving the contradictions between humans and nature. Critics noted that Etzler promised big, but his thinking followed a well-recognized logic and depended, at least in some sense, on the discoveries of others. More than that, predictions of a marvelous future did not surprise many people in the 1830s, and Etzler managed to come off as a pragmatist, articulating defined steps for how to bring it all about. Etzler, however, pursued something beyond the mechanically pragmatic.

•

Improvement of our condition is, and ought to be, our continual aim as long as we live. It behooves not to rational men to abandon their improvement to chance, or to the feeble inefficient efforts of individuals, but to seek and employ the means for it in the best way that is in their power. Man, as an individual, is weak; and whatever his means or abilities be, they are always very limited in comparison to those of many men joined in one body . . . The title of our union shall be: Association for the improvement of the human condition.   —*J. A. Etzler*

Socialist reform in the nineteenth century aimed to mend the dislocation so many people felt as they became wage earners. Though capitalism opened a sphere of human freedom where people could own property and act for themselves, it also made them dependent on money in order to live. The men, women, and children who stood behind power looms, risking injury, breathing fibers, losing their hearing in the noise, all for one dollar a day, did not experience a rush of freedom just because they possessed the right to sell their labor. No one wanted American cities to look like Manchester, England, where, in 1831, four hundred steam engines operated, consuming an estimated seventy thousand pounds of coal every hour. The city also consumed its citizens. Families returned home after ten-hour shifts to reeking tenements. Lacking water or sanitation, sleeping in beds of moldy straw and rags, starving on their wages, these working poor became the first people to be trapped in an economic system that failed to reconcile "national wealth" with the human misery it caused.[43] Americans strained to apply the ideals of 1776 to the unprecedented material realities of 1846. "There are food, clothing and comfortable habitations enough, in every civilized nation," expounded *The Phalanx*, "to feed, clothe, and protect all its people . . . yet the mass of the People everywhere, are miserable, ill fed, half-clothed, ignorant and debased beings."[44] Loss of economic freedom in a society that celebrated political freedom, dependence within memory of the birth of independence, poverty next to wealth—these became the contradictions of capitalism.

What began as a relationship between landlords and tenants in seventeenth-century England had, by the 1820s, become the dominant economic system in the United States. Few people denounced capitalism; instead, they denounced the uneven accumulation of wealth that they saw undermining democracy. The fierce rhetoric of the first labor movement in the United States made clear that the owners of capital did not share a "harmony of interests" with factory operatives. Seth Luther of Rhode Island addressed the mechanics of Brooklyn on the Fourth of July, 1836, roaring, "The workingmen struggle on against the wind and tide of what is called national prosperity, at the same time the employers in many cases strain every nerve to reduce our wages

still lower. If the workingman complains he finds an indict-
ment for conspiracy thrust in his teeth."[45] In *The Working
Man's Manual* (1831), Stephen Simpson attacked the propa-
ganda of progress: "From the earliest epochs of civilized society . . . the *producers* of wealth have, with few exceptions, and
little variation, been degraded to the condition of slaves,
serfs, vassals, or servants."[46] The contradictions seemed to be
mounting.

Idealists set out to resolve the contradictions, but as much
as they hated wage slavery they admired the powerful human
combinations that capitalism created. Why not take the organization and machinery of capital and put them into the
service of an equitable society? Make the factories work for
the workers! Seen through lenses ground by Karl Marx,
however, socialism and capitalism confronted each other in
a fight to the death. "The proletarians cannot become masters of the productive forces of society," he wrote in *The
Communist Manifesto* (1848), "except by abolishing their
own previous mode of appropriation." Capitalist appropriation stood on one leg: private property. Abolish that, and
capital—money—and the market itself would all collapse. But
go back to Marx's time and most other idealist thinkers preferred to fiddle with the system rather than abolish it. Brisbane seized upon Association as an enlightened way of
making people rich that he assumed would eventually lead to
a more humanitarian society. The organizational form that
Brisbane favored coupled a collective form of private property
with cooperative labor.

Brisbane and Fourier embraced the joint-stock company,
the common way of pooling capital by issuing shares. As
Etzler described it, "There are many enterprises of roads,
canals, manufactories &c. executed in our country, at ex-
penses of millions of dollars, which were brought up by vol-

untary associations with shares of 50 dollars and less." Fourier himself made a cosmic accounting of its benefits. Shares would "effect a Unity of the Individual with the collective interest . . . Render real Estate movable property, saleable and convertible at will and without loss . . . Unite the interests of Labour and Capital . . . and prevent the unjust and tyrannical control which the Few . . . now exercise over the destitute Multitude." The joint-stock company solved a nettlesome problem. Shares took the communism out of communal settlement by allowing families and individuals to enter and exit without undermining the organizational structure—an ideal compromise between modern mobility and the desire for belonging. The phalanx did away with individual settlement while preserving individual ownership. Brisbane made his position perfectly clear, especially to his more conservative constituency in the NRA: "Vested rights in property cannot be touched without undermining the fabric of society, and producing injustice, confusion, and, perhaps, bloodshed."[47]

Did Fourierists want to undermine the fabric of society? Not really. Unlike Marx, American Fourierists sought equality without revolution, an end to poverty without class warfare. Fourier offered to protect the poor from the rich by guaranteeing that "capitalists would no longer be able to spoliate and oppress the labouring population," but he fully expected that class would continue to exist in his new world, even suggesting that bourgeoisie and proletariat form separate associations. The goal was harmony and happiness, not redistribution. Promising plush returns, Brisbane urged capitalists to join him: "If Capitalists understood the system of Association, they would feel no repugnance in investing their property in the partnership." Fourierists marveled at the liquidity of real estate, especially that quality of modernity that gave people "the power of rendering real estate a transferable and circulating medium, which can be converted at will and without loss into money." So while Brisbane and Fourier attempted to move beyond the capitalist notion of civil society by insisting that human economic organization must evolve into another form, they really proposed what amounted to a more compassionate version of the same.[48]

We tend to exaggerate the differences between socialism and capitalism as utopian visions. The one predicted a world to come, when people would join hands without greed or hatred. The other affirmed the redemptive power of individuals to enrich themselves and society through the self-regulating market. But during the first half of the century, the two spoke a surprisingly similar language. Political economists could always mask their mysticism by gesturing to apparent things—the production of cotton and textiles or the balance of trade. In fact, they unveiled a future as arresting in its breadth as anything Etzler or Fourier imagined. The French writer Frédéric Bastiat became one of the key figures in the conception of social harmony, the idea that "all men's impulses, when motivated by legitimate self-interest, fall into a harmonious social pattern." He mocked socialists as fantasists who "conjure up a society out of their imagination." But Bastiat conjured a bit himself: "If man's wants are not fixed quantities, but progressive, capable of growth like the inexhaustible desires on which they constantly feed, we must conclude . . . that Nature has placed in man and about him unlimited and constantly increasing means of satisfaction."[49]

This is Providence again. Bastiat, along with almost every political economist at mid-century, imagined nature to be a manifestation of the infinitude of God. William Atkinson, a British statistician and political economist, attacked Malthus for asserting that while life abounds on earth, there isn't

enough room or nourishment for every seed or species to
survive. Atkinson shot back: "In one short sentence he calls
in question and condemns the arrangement and providence
of God." The most pragmatic thinkers of the time, including
Parson Malthus himself, came to a dead end with their reflex-
ive conception of God. If God created the world, they said,
then God must intend for us to do what we want with it. Bastiat spoke much like neoliberals today who hold to a utopian
view best described by Karl Polanyi and the political philosopher John Gray. "In a global free market," writes Gray, "war
and tyranny will disappear. Humanity will advance to unprecedented heights." Providence has underwritten the liberal conception of the world from the time of Adam Smith to
that of George W. Bush. By linking rights and the free market
to nature (and thus to Nature's God), liberalism attempted to
lift them out of politics when it was the nation-state that established them both. Economic liberals also conjured a world
to come in which labor exercised against the eternal substance of the earth would yield capital eternally.[50]

In his essay "The Young American," Ralph Waldo Emerson looked past low wages, child labor, and the twelve-hour
workday to something that filled his lungs with purer air—the
joint-stock company. Emerson seized it as an example of social harmony in the service of universal prosperity. Like Bastiat, he held that economic combination grew out of basic
human desires and aspirations. "The Community is only the
continuation of the same movement which made the joint-
stock companies for manufactures, mining, insurance, bank-
ing, and so forth." Emerson sounded like the president of the
local chamber of commerce: "Gentlemen, the development
of our American internal resources, the extension to the ut-
most of the commercial system, and the appearance of new
moral causes which are to modify the state, are giving an as-

pect of greatness to the Future, which the imagination fears to open."[51] The idealism that seized upon the material world crossed every political line. Progress blurred the distinctions, blended all points of view, and resolved every contradiction into a synthesis romantic and material, ideal and real.

In this way, growth became everyone's favorite social program. Fourierists such as Etzler put forward the very philosophy now embraced by politicians and development agencies around the world—that the way to level the classes, uplift the poor, and create societies free of social conflict is to generate wealth.

•

The book is addressed at once to the Government of the United States, to the American Nation, and to all civilized nations and governments . . . It would be of the happiest consequence for the whole human race, if the unavoidable revolution of the human condition . . . would originate in the United States.

—*J. A. Etzler*

Etzler wrote to President Andrew Jackson in February 1833, but Jackson had other things on his mind. South Carolina threatened to secede over the Tariff of 1828, and both sides prepared armies in an escalating standoff over the authority of federal law. Had the president read the short missive from his admirer in Pittsburgh, he would have encountered a fellow believer in the democratizing power of the state. Jackson represented the triumph of popular government over historical forces that had always opposed it. He came into office almost immediately after some of the states, in an unprecedented diffusion of political power, extended voting rights to free white men of legal age. Jackson also believed in the geographical expansion of the United States into lands controlled by Indians. Etzler must have seen in Jackson the personification of progress, the liberation of wilderness from savagery, and the fire of democracy from which he could steal a flame.

Etzler's faith went back not to Thomas Jefferson, but to Hegel, who called the state the collective embodiment of "the Idea of Spirit in the external manifestation of human Will and its Freedom." No other subject in *Paradise* distinguishes it from other utopian tracts like its author's gestures to the United States. For while other seekers after material progress called the advance of freedom inevitable, Etzler recognized the role of government in instituting it as policy. The very concept of growth implies a nation-state to set goals for it, legislate in favor of it, and intervene in trade and diplomacy to encourage it. The publishing of statistics, the funding of internal improvements, the establishment of central banks, and the assertion of free-trade agreements—no market did these things, and they could not be accounted for by individuals maximizing their self-interest. Twenty-first-century readers cannot recall a time when governments did not manage economies, but that notion has a history.

Before the eighteenth century, the common understanding of national wealth was that it came from trade. No one engaged in trade more successfully than the Dutch. They became a world power in the seventeenth century by streamlining their commercial connections, accumulating bullion from Spain, and dominating the Baltic traffic in linens.[52] The Dutch model, however, never resulted in an exportable system or a set of principles about the wealth of nations. Adam Smith came up with universal principles, a set of categories and relationships that applied to all people everywhere, not to the conditions of specific countries at specific times. Smith said that wealth came from the ways that societies produced things, from divisions of labor. He focused on the process. This made Smith very famous, but not very useful. He said, "The great object of the political economy of every country, is to increase the riches and power of that country"—but every country was different. He said, "The great commerce of every civilized society, is that carried on between the inhabitants of the town and those of the country"—yet how would that help Belgians or Bolivians make policy?[53]

Germans are not often recognized for their school of political economy, but they had one—a way of thinking that gave states primary responsibility for enhancing the public welfare. While Smith argued for limits on state power over the marketplace, Germans emphasized the careful management of tax revenue and the development of internal resources. The career of one reformer looms large here, a career Etzler would have known about. Friedrich List taught administration at the University of Tübingen when, in 1817, he began to advocate his own version of a North Atlantic Free Trade Agreement. List didn't envision an empire; he made the even more startling proposition that Germany become a single economy. He spoke out against the internal duties that made trade among the thirty-nine German states like that between independent nations—sluggish and bureaucratic. But the king of Württemberg liked things just the way they were. He punished List by dismissing him from the university, accusing him of treason, and sentencing him to ten months of hard labor. In 1824, after six months of his brutal term, List was released on condition that he emigrate to the United States. He arrived in Philadelphia in 1825 and stayed five years.

In Pennsylvania, List began to outline a new political economy. He rejected Smith's abstractions in favor of the particular conditions that created economic progress in the United States. "The condition of this nation," he said, "cannot be compared with the condition of any other nation. The same kind of government and same structure of society were never seen before; nor such general and equal distribution of property, of instruction, of industry, of power and wealth; nor similar accomplishments in the gifts of nature, bestowing upon this people natural riches and advantages of the north, of the south, and of the temperate climates, all the advantages of vast sea shores and of an immense unsettled continent." List believed in the genius of a nation, that its industrial and commercial fate could be read in its geographical position—temperate or torrid—as well as in the specific natural resources that lay within its borders. He asked a simple question: "What kind of science is that which sheds no light upon the path which practice must follow?"[54] Smith's labor theory of value might have described conditions in England, but other factors, some having to do with geography and not social organization, better explain Dutch primacy.

List had one important American influence. As an economic nationalist, he linked himself to the first economic nationalist, Alexander Hamilton. At a time when Smith held sway over just about every theorist in Europe and North America, Hamilton came up with a pragmatic philosophy. He regarded the United States as an underdeveloped country and favored policies intended to increase its manufacturing, extend its political and commercial influence over the frontier, and create financial institutions that would lend it money. His "Report on the Subject of Manufactures" reads like a foundation report written for the Washington administration. In it, Hamilton makes the argument that manufacturing should be given "the extraordinary patronage of Government." Government listened, and it was Hamilton—more than any other political economist—who most influenced the subsequent broadening of the executive branch and the financial powers of the government. The American System, the Federal Reserve Bank, the IRS, and the Bureau of Reclamation—to name just a few—aimed to develop the resources of the United States, all stemming from Hamiltonian thinking.

Although government remained almost undetectable in economic life in the early nineteenth century, a few imagined a larger role for it. Henry Clay of Kentucky and John C. Calhoun of South Carolina, two of the framers of that first plan for national development known as the American System, led the way. A protective tariff to encourage domestic manufacturing would encourage rapid innovation in the mechanical arts, send Americans to find value in their own natural resources, and increase domestic consumption. A national bank would promote a single currency and fund internal improvements. A canal system would bring population and trade to the interior and link farmers to markets. List tended to idealize the beneficent state (as Hegel did), and Americans expressed his same sense of genius and destiny. List predicted that the nation would one day count fifty million inhabitants in one hundred states, all of them busy clearing land for wheat. The fertility of its people, stemming from the fertility of its soils, would give the United States power to dominate the world economy. A speaker addressing the American Institute in New York City made the same point: "We shall be the most powerful nation on the globe . . . Let, then, this sense of national greatness be cultivated and based on a foundation nobler and safer than preeminence in war—a superiority in all that can exalt the labor of the human hand."[55] From that time forward, economic growth became conflated with American influence abroad and the capacity of politicians to maintain affluence at home.

•

Putting it all together, Etzler's *Paradise* is a mosaic of the materialist thinking pervasive in the Atlantic World during the previous half century. The result was an oddly plausible utopia: cheap energy and a land regime that traced indelible patterns across the continent by removing American Indians and eradicating wildlife, leading to a soaring human population that would soon live by consuming manufactured products, all financed by joint-stock companies and protected by a government that encouraged growth. All the elements of *Paradise*, and some others, coalesced into the first phenomenon of economic growth in the United States. For although growth had existed for a long time before, as population doubled and settlers entered frontiers, only in the 1820s did Americans begin to realize that a different kind of existence had overtaken them.

By the 1830s, people from Lowell to Pittsburgh began to live differently from the way they had before. Young men performed farmwork for wages, as cash transactions came to mediate all aspects of material life. Families consumed things from outside the household that they once made for themselves. Factories began to turn out textiles, resulting in clothing that could be purchased by a widening sector of the population at a decreasing cost. Amazed by the turn of events in only a few decades, people began to record and measure the change. In 1803, four cotton mills operated in the United States. In 1809, there were eighty-seven. In 1810, Ohio, a wilderness twenty-four years before, produced two million yards of cloth. In 1811, 80,000 spindles turned out cloth throughout New England and New York, representing $4.8 million in capital, employing 500,000 men and 500,000 women and children. The next year, 80,000 spindles turned within thirty miles of Providence, Rhode Island.[56] It is possible to reconstruct GDP for the United States in these years, and the picture is stunning. Nominal GDP—that is, GDP as people at the time would have known it—increased from $700,000 in 1820 to $1.5 billion in 1840. It more than doubled in twenty years. Per capita GDP increased from $73 in

1820 to $97 in 1837, the year a bank panic set off a five-year depression, when GDP fell. After that, it took off again, climbing to $112 in 1847 and $144 in 1855. Real GDP (measured in current dollars) increased 269 percent between 1830 and 1860.[57]

When George Tucker of Virginia published *Progress of the United States in Population and Wealth* (1843), he digested all six federal censuses, using them to construct the most comprehensive early description of GDP. Tucker was the first analyst of growth in the United States—the first statistically capable person to look at the causes of wealth and record their changes. He lent evidence to the general sense of upsurge. "Comparing the same articles of manufacture in 1810 and 1840, the increase, from $59,574,660 to $186,079,592, is 212 per cent in thirty years, or a decennial increase of 46 percent . . . The number employed in 1820 was 36,705 men, 5,812 women, and 13,779 children—in all 56,296. The whole number of persons employed in 1840 was 455,668— that is, as 100 to 809; which supposes the extraordinary decennial increase of 284 per cent. After making the most liberal deduction from this estimate for the omissions in the returns of 1820, the remainder shows an advancement in this branch of industry that is without example."[58] Population rose by 30 percent every ten years from 1790 to 1840, without counting immigration, but wealth rose even faster because labor efficiency exploded from preindustrial levels. As Tucker noted, "By means of cheaper and quicker modes of transportation, much of that labour which, in every country is expended, not in producing, but in transferring products from place to place, is saved and rendered directly productive."

This accelerated productivity meant that people spent less of their incomes on clothing, in particular, freeing income to be spent on other things. A rising standard of living—the quality and quantity of goods available to people for their greater health and comfort—is how people experienced economic growth and how they understood its benefits. They ate from porcelain plates, not wooden platters; bought lanterns at the dry-goods store rather than make their own candles; and preferred the woolen coats stitched for them to the frumpy homespun they once took as a sign of republican independence. A speaker addressing the American Institute admitted, "We gaze with astonishment upon the rapid succession of wonderful events which pass before our eyes . . . The most sanguine, enthusiastic mind, in its dreamy visions, can scarcely imagine a more prosperous growth, or a more rapid development of resources." A correspondent, having visited the mills at Lowell, Massachusetts, said simply, "A new and better social existence is being extended to the race."[59]

Growth became the essence of society itself—so essential to present contentment and future stability that it took over the full meaning of civilization. Anthropologists define *civilization* (to the extent that they use the term at all) as any region of linked settlements that share a common language and religious beliefs. The word merely distinguishes those who led a settled existence from those who did not. But by the nineteenth century, *civilization* increasingly referred to industrialism and the wealth it generated. Ezra Seaman, author of a popular book on the subject, asserted, "Civilization and wealth generally advance together. *Industry and property therefore lie at the very foundation of civilization; without which it cannot exist*; and it progresses in proportion to the advance a people make in productive industry." The expansion Seaman contemplated had no complicating factors, no negative effects whatsoever. He wrote from inside the ideal world that fused growth with human destiny. "The laws of nature are uniform," cheered Seaman, but people have it in their power to "alter the face of nature, and convert the ores and mineral substances in the bowels of the earth, . . . as well as nature's laws, into instruments and mechanical powers." The small human animal would subdue the earth, convert its resources, increase the yields of agriculture, transport them, exchange them, accumulate capital—all allowing him to "increase his capital and wealth, and . . . multiply his comforts with still greater and greater rapidity."[60]

A sober reality formed the flip side of Seaman's elation: there was no turning back. A speaker at the American Institute addressed a crowd stunned by the financial panic of 1837. He told them that modern society had no alternatives to material progress. "The manufacture of wool, iron, cotton, and like articles of daily necessity must and will go on," he gravely intoned. "Their magnitude—the necessity for a division of labour, their inseparable connection with us, as a free, independent people—the manner in which they are interwoven with our social and political structure, imparting to it its great and growing strength—their union with agriculture, fostering and warming it into prosperity—all prove to us, that we may as well tear from the tender vine its support, under the delusion that it will rise up by its own vigor . . . as to divorce the manufacturing and mechanical branches of industry from the agricultural . . . Mechanical and manufacturing industry have sent down everywhere, thousands of strong roots, which can never be torn up without bringing with them the foundations of all abiding prosperity!"[61] Manufacturing had become "the machinery of civilization." Society had become embedded in economy—not the other way around.

Southerners didn't share the same optimism. They subscribed to a darker view, more deeply informed by Malthus, more tightly pinned to an agrarian rather than an industrial economy. The chemist and political economist Thomas Cooper denied that productivity would ever increase very much. "To all agricultural improvement," he warned his students, "there must be a term where it ends—a maximum." A professor of literature saw a struggle taking place in the landscape as space dedicated to domesticated plants and animals encroached on the weedy parts of the world. Expansion followed inevitably under pressure of population, he said, and in this battle, "the weeds, however productive, the wild animals, however prolific, are exterminated. One order is supported only by the extinction of others." He concluded, "In theory at least, the time must at last arrive when the failure of land, and the attainment of its maximum of production, must be an insuperable bar to any further advancement." Southerners did not reject the basic premise that growth equaled civilization; they just looked at the problem from their own key factors of production—slave labor and virgin forest—and tended to resign themselves to some degree of decline. They felt limitations more immediately, and this became part of their resentment against the North.[62]

Statistical measurement focused attention on the output and cost of production. It became allied to technological innovation and government policies because these directly affected what eventually became the assessment of GDP. Highly concentrated energy and the machines that turned heat into work lowered the cost of making things, moved us farther and faster, compressing our sense of distance and space, and within a century made food so cheap that what had once been the continual obsession of peasants and pharaohs—starvation—nearly vanished. The odd consequence of this revolutionized existence was that it became closed to feedback from anything outside of itself, except in the form of fluctuating prices. Economic growth functioned as an open system, one that interpreted stasis as decline, when below the soil and under the sea, life continued to follow a thermodynamic process, as organisms absorbed matter and energy for a time before giving them up, in a closed system of growth and disintegration.

The expectation of proliferating goods, of more and more people employed in a widening economy, committed the people of industrial societies to policies of wealth creation that had no way of communicating with the changes those policies caused in actual environments. Growth became the symbol of social happiness, the conduit of health and safety, presenting us with an unprecedented quandary. Even as it offered a better existence, it was running on a collision course with its own unexamined assumptions.

•

Etzler did not surface again until 1840, when he sailed into New York harbor on March 3 aboard the schooner *Lexington* from Port-au-Prince, Haiti.[63] After leaving the Old Northwest in 1834, he most likely set out for Texas, the Gulf, and then the Caribbean, where he probably experimented in the extraction of sugar from cane and fruit, something he later claimed could feed the world. He might have traveled to France to visit a Fourierist community in Dijon. He looked for new adherents everywhere, but as he later wrote, "I could not find any attention worth mentioning, neither among learned nor unlearned, nor of our government."[64] Dried out from the sun, without a follower but still certain that his name and fortunes must rise—and now almost fifty years old—he came to New York to try again. In April he read about a celebration to be held marking the birthday of Charles Fourier. That is where he met Conrad Stollmeyer, the socialist businessman who played a crucial role in the rest of

Etzler's life, who stood by him as all the strands of an earthly paradise seemed to wind together and then unravel. Over the next seven years they built fantastic machines and converted thousands of weary English laborers, who dedicated their meager shillings to a great utopian project. Only one element remained. Human improvement pointed to a geographical address, a place stipulated by nature as the location of historical culmination. There would be a gathering of all humanity—in the tropics.

CHAPTER THREE

Utopia *Means "No Place"*

こんこんこん

E ngland and Venezuela are forty-eight hundred miles apart. The most direct line between them crosses the Tropic of Cancer at 25° north latitude and keeps falling southwest to a point 7° above the equator. It is not true that the tropics have no winter and no seasonal change, but temperatures there do not fluctuate as they do in temperate climates. The summer sun is closer, its rays falling to Earth almost vertically. While fair-skinned people burn within minutes of exposure, the flora soaks the rays in, producing fruit of great size and sweetness—blue passionflower, camu-camu, mamey sapote, Malabar chestnut, and guabilla—that stunned those from the drizzle and frost of northern Europe. The tropics vexed and maddened them as the region thwarted their attempts to press upon it their designs for mastery. Etzler had his own designs for the tropics: he believed that they belonged to all humanity and that the energy concentrated there would fuel an agriculture rich enough to sustain one trillion people. "We are on the eve of the most eventful period of mankind," he observed. "Migrations of millions from north to south will soon take place, and new nations and empires will be founded by them, superior in every respect to any known in history."

The weight of history bore down on Conrad Stollmeyer. He had come out of the same context as Etzler and pursued his own idealist vision quest. Born in Ulm in 1813, he attended university, where he read the authors of the radical Enlightenment and evaded conscription into the army of the king of Württemberg by faking poor health. As he wrote years later about the Bavaria he hated, "If I had remained in Germany, without a doubt I would have mixed up in politics and would either have been shot, put to the gallows or put in prison for the duration of my life." Stollmeyer emigrated to Philadelphia, arriving in March 1836. He helped open a bookshop and founded a socialist organization, Die Demokratische Union. Animated by the desire for an exemplary community, he joined the German Settlement Society

Conrad Stollmeyer. A utopian businessman, he became Etzler's most ardent follower and interpreter, as well as the chief apologist for the disaster in Venezuela. (Courtesy of the Stollmeyer family)

and contributed financially to the purchase of 11,300 acres in the Gasconade River valley of Missouri. He had another reason to quit Philadelphia in 1838. As a member of the executive committee of the Pennsylvania Anti-Slavery Society, he felt his life threatened by a mob that burned the society's meeting hall during a nightlong rampage. Socialism in Missouri, however, didn't work out. Returning to Philadelphia the next year, he recommitted himself as a publisher, attaching his imprint to books espousing progressive philosophies.[1]

Then he met Etzler, and everything stopped. Fourier's birthday party must have been windy with conjecture, but here stood a practical man of science with an intense and distant gaze who claimed that he could unify physics and economy, turn sunshine into money. The time for actualization had arrived—for both of them. For the next seven years, Stollmeyer did almost nothing but think of Etzler, talk of Etzler, publish and promote Etzler, and rearrange every personal detail of his life to accommodate Etzler. Charismatic leaders often depend on dedicated interpreters. Charisma is not the ability to communicate, and it is certainly not the quality of being well liked. It is the capacity to impose an idea on others that they internalize. Charismatic leaders make people see the world as they do—but not always by making reasoned arguments. They foretell obscurely, speak in poetry, and declare irreducible truths without evidence. They don't have friends, since everyone serves the instrumental purpose of advancing their views. So Aaron spoke for his brother Moses and performed the rituals that translated prophecy into religious practice. Jesus needed the disciples to elaborate and spread his message. Sherlock Holmes depended on Dr. Watson to act as a catalyst for his thinking about crime. Stollmeyer did this for Etzler. He performed the rituals.[2]

The first product of their relationship was a book: *The New World, or, Mechanical System: To Perform the Labours of Man and Beast by Inanimate Powers, That Cost Nothing, for Producing and Preparing the Substances of Life* (1841). It contained the first complete description of the Satellite as well as Etzler's call to rethink political revolution in favor of his system. "Of what avail is any social reform, when the desires for the requisites of happiness of the individual must remain unsatisfied; when the contentment of poverty is demanded as a virtue or a necessity, while the rich neighbors tantalize the poor?" Violent revolution was just as ineffective, Etzler believed, since the goal was not merely a change of government but true liberation. To the poor, struggling masses seeking amelioration of their condition, Etzler held out "peace, wealth, happiness, not at the expense of your fellow creatures, but by creative means applied to the, as yet, unused rich resources of nature." He continually challenged the doubters—"I defy the world to disprove my facts"—now in a diction smoothed by his interpreter. Stollmeyer wrote it all down, cleaned up the German-into-English awkwardness, and put it into print.[3]

They divided their tasks. Stollmeyer moved to secure the inventor's exclusive rights over his inventions. Etzler received patents for the Satellite (described to the patent office as a locomotive propelled by stationary power, patent number 2396, December 23, 1841) and the Naval Automaton (a means of "navigating and propelling vessels by action of wind and waves," patent number 2533, April 1, 1842).[4] Rather than give these designs to all the world, he now owned them. The visionary, however, had already headed west and south. A collector and critic of utopian experiments named A. J. MacDonald just missed him in New Harmony, Indiana, in 1841. A friend of MacDonald's reported that he had spent a few days with Etzler on a flatboat on the Ohio River, reporting Etzler's attempt to "burn the brushwood in the vicinity of Louisville by means of 'burning mirrors.' " After that, little was heard of Etzler until 1843, when he turned up again in Pennsylvania. Still, throughout all his frenetic and compulsive travel, he remained in contact with Stollmeyer.

Stollmeyer left for London in the summer of 1841. He had contacts there and felt repelled by the many factors that made the United States a poor location for launching a large-scale project. The open West tended to send people outward and away from one another. They collected in towns and cities for the purpose of making money, feeling that they had already found a better life than what they had known in the East. In Britain, Stollmeyer found a recently dispossessed, socially abused, and increasingly activist working class. Socialism thrived there. Robert Owen had returned from Pennsylvania in 1827 to found the London Co-operative Society. English laborers and artisans pursued enlightenment and equality in the Barnsbury Park Community (an experimental garden cooperative), the Westminster Co-operative Society (providing land for the unemployed), and the Philosophic Land Association, among many others.[5] Stollmeyer started out by publishing regular missives in the *Northern Star*, a Chartist newspaper, meant to provoke interest and gather support for Etzler's eventual arrival. Everyone seemed to be rethinking the nature and purpose of work. Stollmeyer tried to cut through the question (and grab some attention) by challenging the "erroneous notion . . . that the people want work; that man ought to work . . . The people *do not want work*. Work is not the *end* . . . The end is provisions, happiness, the satisfaction of all our rational desires."[6] He joined the lecture circuit, toting around models of the great inventions for all who cared to learn, but he strained to be heard.

If he really wanted to make a splash and direct all eyes on Etzler's ideas, he would have to make the powers of the earth actually do something.

In the fall of 1842, Stollmeyer began building a Naval Automaton with the questionable technical assistance of Hugh Doherty, editor of *The London Phalanx*. Doherty, a believer, called Etzler's proposed Satellite "astounding in its promises" and affirmed of the inventor that "whatever he describes, in principle, he could perform in fact." Drawings from the Automaton's patent application show a rotating sail on the bow and a stern wind wheel, but the real power came from the motion of ocean swells against three floats submerged below the keel. As these floats undulated, they pulled cables and turned wheels that moved paddles connected to the deck. By December, Stollmeyer felt confident enough to pilot the completed boat across the Channel. Doherty had even packed his razor and a few personal items into the cabin, thinking that a trip to France would make a fine demonstration and a little vacation, but Stollmeyer first needed to test the craft in the Thames. The current did not play along. Rather than push the floats upward, generating power, the water flowed over them. As the sails continued to move the boat forward, the drag plunged it into the icy December river. Stollmeyer jumped for his life. He then spent £15 to raise it and another £30 to repair it. He insisted that the floats could be perfected and the Channel crossing accomplished, but friends were doubtful. One with a little wit asked "if France lay at the bottom of the sea."[7]

Embarrassed but not defeated, Stollmeyer made plans for an even grander project: a floating island. In a letter to *Mechanics' Magazine* written from London and dated October 1843, he announced that he had experimented with Etzler's blueprints (by building a model) and would begin to

J. A. Etzler.   Sheet 2, 4 Sheets.

Sails & Rigging.

Nº 2,533.   Patented Apr. 1, 1842.

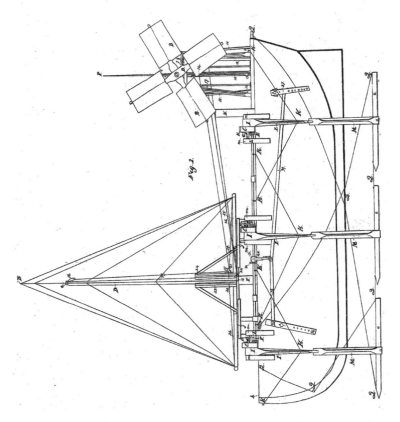

The Naval Automaton. Etzler believed that energy could be captured in ways that might free people from the clutches of factory owners, radically increasing their mobility so that they could cultivate the earth. The Naval Automaton received a patent, which suggests that government examiners considered it a plausible design. (From Etzler's patent application, United States Patent Office)

construct a series of "vast floating bodies, which cannot sink under any circumstances, and may be propelled by the united powers of wind, waves, and steam." The vessel (if that's how to describe it) would have far outdrawn the largest ships of the time. In July the steamship *Great Britain* thundered out of dry dock—six masts over an iron hull 322 feet long, moving under 1,000 horsepower. But Etzler's floating island would be 600 yards long and 200 yards wide in the center. Beneath a solid bottom seven feet thick, a set of timber supports *thirty yards thick* would run diagonally, forming an X. The plans included houses, streets, an observatory, a dining room, and machinery. It would be fast enough to chase down the *Great Britain*, and Stollmeyer offered it for the Empire's defense.[8] But before he could begin construction, his priorities changed. Etzler, he learned, had shipped for London.

•

Henry David Thoreau wrote a long essay on *Paradise* for *The United States Magazine and Democratic Review* in 1843, the year Etzler moved to England. Two years later, Thoreau would build a cabin on Walden Pond, conducting an experiment in many ways the direct opposite of Etzler's. Though Thoreau more or less agreed with Etzler that humans had not made the fullest use of the powers of nature, he sneered at technological schemes. "We will not be imposed upon by this vast application of forces," he said, and countered that "most things will have to be accomplished still by the application called Industry." Thoreau cast progress differently, as a moral improvement, and he doubted that the "new means" would do anything toward that end. "Sometimes, we confess, we are so degenerate as to reflect with pleasure on the days when men were yoked like cattle, and drew a crooked stick for a plough." The two had nowhere to meet. Thoreau managed to appreciate and dismiss Etzler's project at the same time. "Mr. Etzler," he wrote, "has more of the practical than usually belongs to so bold a schemer, so resolute a dreamer. Yet his success is in theory, and not in practice, and he feeds our faith rather than contents our understanding . . . His castles in the air fall to the ground, because they are not built lofty enough; they should be secured to heaven's roof." When Thoreau observed, "It would seem . . . that there is a transcendentalism in mechanics as well as in ethics," he nailed his subject. In the end, he did not complain that *Paradise* aimed too high, but that it aimed *too low*: "The chief fault of this book is, that it aims to secure the greatest degree of gross comfort and pleasure merely."

Thoreau was not Etzler's only reviewer that year. Luke James Hansard anticipated Etzler's arrival in England, writing of the powers Etzler proposed to employ: "We have not the most distant conception of their magnitude, or of the measure in which they may be adapted to the wants and necessities of man." But how would it play in England? "Mr. Etzler's ideas . . . will never suit our English head; and though his plans are admirable, and worthy of profound investigation . . . John Bull will turn up his nose at them." He offered the tantalizing prediction that "if any plain practical mechanic will take his Drawings, make a Machine, and show the people how to use it, and what it will effect when used; I am positive it would tend more to spread Mr. Etzler's fame and realize his conceptions than all the books he has written ever can or will do."[9] The *Church of England Review* noticed "the tendency of men in this day to Universalism in the region of physical nature." The editors felt a surge coming that would elevate Catholicism and all humanity. "Progress, progress is the law, and every effort made against it will only tend to hasten a consummation . . . In things outward, in things mental, in things spiritual, there are struggles going on." Great efforts always come along with "dust and confusion," they said, but "such efforts can never take place without leading to some great result." Etzler's *Mechanical System* provided their central example.[10] By the time the inventor arrived in England, he enjoyed surprising notoriety, especially among socialists. But he never set out simply to invent things. He wanted followers, and he found them in the working class.

•

Anticipation among a small number of ardent utopians built to near messianic devotion as the practical visionary stepped into the city of London. He immediately published a tract, *Emigration to the Tropical World*, that became the central text of the organization he founded. A few months later, in October 1844, he called a meeting at his home to organize the Tropical Emigration Society. The thirty-three founding members elected Etzler president and Stollmeyer treasurer, along with six directors. Thomas Powell, a London bookkeeper, served as secretary. Recognizing that Etzler and Stollmeyer had contributed the intellectual and mechanical basis of the organization, the members granted them each one share for every ten issued. After first addressing a large crowd on October 27 at the Parthenium on St. Martin's Lane and facing a rush of interest and popularity, Etzler embarked on a speaking tour of northern England and Scotland. Serious and brooding, in the habit of lecturing in dramatic style, with his body thrust forward, Etzler meant to astound his audiences with working models of the Satellite and the Naval Automaton. He urged and advocated before mechanics institutes, sermonized before the first infant branches of the society in the north of England, and made plans for branches in Germany, France, and the United States.

Back in London by November, he held a congress to settle the constitution and arranged for his journey to Venezuela, "in order to make his surveys . . . before the commencement of the rainy season." He revealed then that he planned to find a location in cooperation with the Venezuelan government. A small number of "pioneers" would follow to build houses and ready a settlement for the arrival of a larger party before the entire society made the passage. The whole scheme depended so completely on Etzler's claims that the Satellite and the Naval Automaton (as the official means of transportation) were written into the constitution. In December the first issue of *The Morning Star, or Herald of Progression* appeared, edited by James Elmslie Duncan, with an opening dedication: "To promote the great end—the one great thing needful—MAN'S PROGRESSION." But everything glowed in the light of the leader: "If any topic has precedence it will be the plans of that greatest of scientific men—ETZLER!"

The subscribers leaked out of British society, the human fallout of an industrial system that made their submission a precondition of their employment. They were the wounded operatives and indebted clerks clinging to wages. A list of the members who eventually took passage for Venezuela included a corn miller, a wool comber, and a carpenter, along with dyers, spinners, mechanics, and an accountant. Thomas Marshall, of the East End of London, was a bookseller. Others who followed included brickmakers, coopers, and common laborers.[11] The English working class suffered so utterly from their degraded and unprotected position that they sought out anything that promised to alleviate their trauma. Friedrich Engels, who walked the same streets Etzler did and wrote

The Condition of the Working Class in England the same year
Etzler published *Emigration to the Tropical World*, captured
the dehumanizing current of poverty and insecurity that
waited outside the factory gates for every workingwoman
and -man: "He knows that every breeze that blows, every
whim of his employer, every bad turn of trade may hurl him
back into the fierce whirlpool from which he has temporarily
saved himself, and in which it is hard and often impossible to
keep his head above water."

These people fell into the vortex of English capitalism.
Over the previous two centuries, landlords had secured the
legal right to claim as private property lands that had lain in
common for time out of mind, throwing peasant farmers into
the labor market. The first industrial factories fired up in the
1750s, offering the dispossessed work for wages. As they did
in so many ways and with such dire consequences, liberal theorists looked to nature to justify the new order of things.
They said that the market existed under some unnamed laws
of the universe, a self-regulating, eternally existent, and nearly
mystical mechanism. Because the market—like the oceans—
had no clear point of origin and could never cease to exist,
how could anyone question it? What alternatives to it existed?
Rather than acknowledge the lack of protection so many people suffered, industrialists and their allies in Parliament regarded the consequences of economic growth as necessary
and inevitable. In the words of Karl Polanyi, economic liberalism was a "utopian endeavor," set in motion by ideas "as
extreme and radical as ever inflamed the minds of sectarians."
Though reformers tried to mitigate the damage, "an ava-
lanche of social dislocation . . . came down upon England."
This is why the young Engels, booted and frocked on the
squalid streets, fixed on the hardscrabble life of the industrial
cities as "the real basis and point of departure of all social

movements of the present, because it is the highest and most unconcealed pinnacle of the social misery existing in our day."[12]

Given the daunting opposition, it is no wonder that thousands of poor artisans chose escape over resistance. Etzler showed them a way out of their hellhole. He told them that they lived not only in an inferior society but also in "the inferior half of the globe with a periodical death of nature," forcing people to perpetual labor and conflict "for the poor pittance of their wants." Climate could be social destiny. Increase the energy coming from the sky, and you eliminate conflict. *The Morning Star* beat the same drum. In the tropics, these poor artisans, "hitherto the despised of all men, and the befouled of calumny, will speedily make themselves the princes of the earth; for *science* shall be their slave." So they debated it in pubs and coffeehouses, they read the full spectrum of socialist newspapers, and a good number of them salted up their banknotes for one share in the people's own joint-stock company, with the promise of a one-way ticket to abundance.[13] But where, exactly, were they going?

Utopia means "no place." Thomas More coined the term, and his own *Utopia* (1516) can be read on more than one level, suggesting that to pursue perfection and happiness for all is really to disappear from lived experience. Samuel Butler published his own sardonic account in *Erewhon* (1872)— "nowhere" (more or less) spelled backward. These were not great endorsements. One problem with the idea of utopia is that by universalizing the qualities of an ideal society, it stubbornly refuses to set down in any actual geography. By definition, it fails to account for the specific conditions of specific places. Put another way, utopia *means "no place" because it means "every place"*—they're really the same.[14] Like the physicists and political economists who argued that life and economy could be understood as an expression of the forces that prevailed throughout the universe, Etzler believed that his own utopia, including his machines, could be established anywhere. Of course, Venezuela was *somewhere*, but Etzler could not be bothered with details. All he needed to know came down to altitude and temperature, to the proportion of mountains to plains—variables he could manipulate. "We know," he concluded, "that the torrid zone is *not* a scorching zone, unfit for man to live."[15] What little Etzler knew, however, only magnified what he imagined.

The partners gathered intelligence from sources that gave them little accurate information about the possible disadvantages of Venezuela. Etzler chose the country because it sustained a republican government that offered settlers freedom of religion while suspending compulsory military service and taxes for fifteen years. By an act of May 1844, the government offered land to immigrants, with no money down for a limited period before requiring purchase. But rather than look hard at known cases of Europeans attempting agricultural settlement, Etzler read less specific accounts, as well as a book by a French explorer named Jean-J. Dauxion-Lavaysse. *The Morning Star* reprinted long sections of his *Description of Venezuela, Trinidad, Margarita, and Tobago* (1820). Members read about trees oozing with edible sap, wild fruits, roots, and leaves easily harvested. Yet Lavaysse also came upon seven thousand Europeans forming a colony that hung on in a "simple and laborious" existence, with nothing "that approaches luxury in their dress, furniture, and houses." No paradise. But when Etzler happened upon contrary stories, he explained them away.[16] These poor wretches didn't have a Satellite and had no knowledge of the abundance around them.

James Duncan, editor of *The Morning Star*, dismissed the

association of the tropics with disease by denying that anyone could even become ill there: "There is no disease, no such thing as coughs or colds, nor do we ever hear of decline, consumption, rheumatism, lumbago, cramp, agues, sore necks, sore throats, swellings, chilblains, O no!" Another expounded, "Sand flies and chigoes, with other tropical insects, are not an insuperable barrier . . . Anybody with a moderate proportion of pluck in him would only laugh at these trivial annoyances." Etzler cited Alexander von Humboldt's observation that one acre of bananas yielded 133 times the nutritional value of an acre of wheat and 44 times that of potatoes. Eating would be a cinch. With food dripping from land known to be "productive of 100 times more than all the rest of the world," the fortunate emigrants would spend their time cultivating their interests.[17] This is why Etzler identified the tropics as the location of all future human progress. It appeared to offer all the material necessary for sustaining civilization, made possible entirely through the intensity of sunlight shining on the green stuff of the earth.

One food seemed to concentrate all the light that beamed from scientific idealism, a substance so dynamic that it invigorated as it fed the body, so nutritive that humans needed little else to survive. The settlers would eat sugar. Etzler and Stollmeyer considered sugar the most direct agricultural manifestation of sunlight; and like sunlight itself, they thought, sugar transcended capitalism and every national trade policy because its potential plenty would make its cost irrelevant. Sugar "is not dependent upon legislative measures of Parliament," wrote Stollmeyer, "but entirely upon the vivifying power of the sun, the productiveness of the soil, and the energies and knowledge of present and future proprietors of sugar plantations." He deemed it "the most important article of food" and claimed to have discovered evidence of its spontaneous formation. "In countries where there is much solar heat and a barren soil, destitute of vegetation, the atmosphere deposits sugar, which granulates:—the manna of the deserts!"[18] It happened in California, he reported, and in North Africa. Apparently, the atmosphere did not deposit sugar on the ground in Venezuela, but no worries. Etzler claimed to have experimented with extracting it from fruit, and he offered to teach the government of Venezuela the technique. For centuries, Caribbean sugar had been produced exclusively by African slaves, but the new means would destroy the plantation economy, spreading revolution and sweetness.

●

The tropics took up more than just geographical space for Europeans. Etzler's beliefs came from a troubled place, where the yearning for paradise became the rationale for colonialism, where nineteenth-century racial science and the nascent study of human origins began to parcel out the globe into continents, each productive of a certain civilization. Etzler would have known of an emerging body of thought that attempted to explain how climate molded society. It was called human geography, and not only did it inform a rising interest in the tropical world, it had distinctive German roots. Hegel himself asserted history's geographical basis, that "in the History of the World, the Idea of Spirit appears in its actual embodiment as a series of external forms." Every world-historical people possessed a "*natural* characteristic" that shaped them as surely as soil and moisture shaped living nature. Each continent suggested a distinct civilization born of environmental qualities.[19] Hegel learned this science from his countrymen, whose theories revealed a secret about progress written in oceans and continents on the apparently disordered globe.

Environmental determinism depicted a world of whole-ness and continuity, an example of the modern desire for sta-ble concepts and simplification amid rising complexity and accelerating change. The discourse on climate by Charles de Secondat, Baron de Montesquieu, in *The Spirit of the Laws* (1748) stands as the most famous early attempt to interpret human behavior as a phenomenon of nature. Montesquieu's ideas found a European and North American elite eager for a code that would help them understand the many peoples re-cently brought under colonial rule. He offered them sooth-ing transparency: "In cold countries, they have very little sensibility for pleasures; in temperate countries they have more; in warm countries their sensibility is exquisite." Nature sliced through complexity and gave Westerners an illusory in-sight into what they experienced as a chaos of foreign cul-tures. The book became a favorite in the rising market for travel literature because its climatic explanations of human characteristics freed travelers, statesmen, and philosophers from having to know anything about the people they met when their sailing ships arrived at ports of call.[20]

The study of comparative human geography dates from the work of Carl Ritter, a contemporary of Alexander von Humboldt and author of the monumental *Erdkunde* (1817–59). Ritter influenced a generation of German ideal-ists, including Hegel and Marx (who attended Ritter's lec-tures at the University of Berlin), by imagining the earth as an eternal structure animated by divine power. Ritter postu-lated that "nations, like men, are formed under a law superior to themselves," which took the form of climate—a set of physical qualities (latitude, elevation, proximity to mountains and oceans) that formed the DNA of societies, explaining their historical patterns. Such a view construed economic de-pression, civil war, and revolution as the epiphenomena of primordial processes. As Ritter's student and emissary to

North America, Arnold Guyot promoted his mentor's expansive conception of geography, spinning out from the landforms of the planet the "incessant mutual actions . . . of inorganic nature upon organized beings, upon man in particular, and upon the successive development of human societies." Guyot set out to capture "the life of the globe," by which he meant the history and destiny of humankind.[21]

That is what the Swiss-born Guyot attempted in a series of lectures at Harvard University in 1849 before joining the faculty of Princeton University. He turned the globe this way and that, amazing his audience by pronouncing a theorem of nations based on temperatures and coastlines. Behold the North: the close proximity of its three masses and its temperate climates leading to ease of communication and the most advanced examples of life. Behold the South: its three masses in oceanic isolation, "shut up in themselves, incapable of reacting upon each other"; stagnant. Guyot believed that the shapes of continents indicated the mental abilities of their human inhabitants. Lacking the peninsulas of Europe, which to him suggested a capacity for complex thought, the southern bodies produced only "the most deformed and degenerate races, and the lowest in the scale of humanity." Thus spake Guyot—the globe his only datum, his sole experiment. Geographers did not invent race as a way of organizing people, but they were among the first to extend it scientific authority. They reasoned that environments differed from place to place, sustaining very different communities of plants and animals. Therefore, by what justification did humans escape this same influence? Or, as Guyot put the question, "If the distribution of the human races on the surface of the globe does not follow the law of the rest of nature, what, then, is the law that regulates it?"[22]

The ether of German idealism permeates Continental geography of the nineteenth century, but with ominous conse-

quences for human freedom. Guyot believed that history and
the earth contained inherent patterns, an embedded logic
that pointed toward the utopian rule of Europeans over
everyone else. He said that the geography of Europe fitted its
people to rule so that they might lead the poor nations of the
global south "into the movement of universal progress and
improvement, wherein mankind should share." Listen to
Guyot and you might hear King Leopold of Belgium ratio-
nalizing the infiltration of the Congo in the 1870s, which resulted in the slaughter and torture of villagers for rubber:
"The races inhabiting [the southern continents] are captives
in the bonds of all powerful nature; they will never break
down the fences that sunder them from us. It is for us, the favored races, to go to them."[23] One of the ironies of the appeal to nature in the late Enlightenment is that although it
ignited movements of political equality, it also asserted the
absoluteness of human differences, toward an immovable system of ranks that no revolution could overturn.

Yet behind Guyot's bizarre misreading of the globe
loomed capitalist necessity. Industrialism in England would
have been impossible without land abroad to furnish it with
hundreds of thousands of pounds of raw cotton coming from
India, the American South, and the Caribbean. Colonies fed
the first industries with materials that allowed the English to
dedicate their own land to food production. Other commodities, some that became definitive of industrialism, came from
the tropics. Venezuela mostly exported cacao before 1810,
but coffee prices began to rise, setting off a surge in planting.
Coffee production tripled during the 1830s until it accounted for a third to half of the country's total exports, a
boom fueled by the clearing of forested land between 3,000
and 6,500 feet above sea level. Sugar, tea, and coffee provided stimulants and calories (especially when combined with
cream or milk) that increased worker productivity and en-

Two views of the tropics. The map depicts the Gulf of Paria in the 1820s, but one way to see how Etzler envisioned South America is through this etching by Johann Moritz Rugendas, a German from Augsburg who traveled the continent from 1834 to 1836. *Virgin Forest* (1835) depicts a rich canopy, a floor dense with ferns, and a general picture of the rain forest dripping with life. Charles Darwin recommended the same engraving to his sister so she would have an accurate image in mind of where he was while on expedition. (Map from *Voyage aux îles de Trinidad, de Tobago, de la Marguerite, et dans diverses parties de Venezuela, dans l'Amérique Meridionale*, by J. J. Dauxion-Lavaysse, Paris, 1813. Etching courtesy of the American Antiquarian Society)

hanced time discipline in the workplace. This use of tea, in particular, was already established by 1800, when English workers spent 5 percent of their income on the dried leaves of an evergreen bush from China. Europeans imported other products from Venezuela, including sugar, cattle hides, and indigo.[24] Within a century, the automobile industry depended on rubber; a Boston company imported bananas for tens of millions of breakfast tables; and in 1913 Royal Dutch Shell shifted its operations to oil deposits discovered near Lake Maracaibo. The tropics—underdeveloped as a mirror image of the development they made possible—financed the economic growth of the twentieth century.

Etzler had read the geographers, and he understood his own errand in the tropics as the redemption of the region under the eventual rule of a civilized race. He regarded the country as culturally blank (neither he nor any of his followers interacted with Venezuelans) and economically underexploited. In his myopic calculations and outrageous conceits, Etzler predicted the capitalists who followed him. But he kept his distance from the environment of Venezuela, carefully avoiding the ecological reality so at odds with his preconceptions. What he did not know, nor could he have, was that of Venezuela's land area (882,000 square kilometers, or about twice the size of California), only 4 percent is considered arable. The other 96 percent consists of the Andes Mountains, Maracaibo Lowlands, Llanos plains, and Guiana Highlands. The partners had no idea that they were about to enter an environment that would give them only the narrowest margins for the kind of subsistence they and their followers practiced, and their foggy thinking prevented them from preparing for it.

•

On February 6, 1845, Etzler sailed for Trinidad from the docks at Gravesend, on the south bank of the Thames. Only at this moment in the story do the surviving documents reveal that he was married. No one recorded the name of the German woman who boarded the brig *James* with him, along with her mother, sister, and brother-in-law, who had arrived in London from Germany just in time to make the voyage. Very likely she had been with him since 1831, never acknowledged. They pulled away at midday, "all in the most excellent spirits," for a passage of more than a month in comfortable, roomy quarters. The boat headed for Madeira under a northeast gale before picking up the trade winds for its southern course. Accompanying the family were two agents of the Tropical Emigration Society, Thomas Carr and Captain Charles Taylor. Carr and Taylor first came to public attention at a tea held some days before the departure, in which three hundred well-wishers toasted the expedition. At the party, Etzler revealed that he had first met Carr in Philadelphia. Carr and Taylor had instructions from the directors to seek a "free grant" from the government of Venezuela—up to seventy thousand acres. The *James* arrived at Port of Spain, Trinidad, around March 21. After studying the topography during the crossing, Etzler, Carr, and Taylor agreed to look on the peninsula of Paria, an east-west strut of land fifty miles long and twenty wide, for an initial settlement, while they approached the government for a larger "main grant" inland.[25]

The search for land had begun. Etzler remained in Trinidad while Carr and Taylor rigged up a boat and set off for Paria, landing first at Guarapiche, a bay at the western tip of the peninsula. The excitable Carr ran around, "cutlass in hand," slashing the foliage aimlessly, covered in sweat. Taylor hunted. They slept outside on boards, sustained by black bread, roasted plantains, and coffee. They decided not to proceed up the Rio Orinoco for fear that the journey would take too long. Returning to Trinidad three weeks later, they told Etzler about a plantation they had found that cost $2,500. Since the financing of the entire venture depended on the government's offer of thousands of acres for next to nothing, the cost astounded Etzler, and no one had a plan to pay for it. They argued, couldn't decide what to do next, and finally agreed to look somewhere else—Angostura, to the east. Etzler hated the idea and wrote, "I packed my things with a heavy heart—the rainy season commenced now—Carr had already a fever . . . but I was crippled in my will and power." Yet Etzler prevailed upon Taylor to give up the plan; instead, he offered to travel alone to Caracas to negotiate directly with the government for a grant. Five weeks had gone by with little to show for it. Etzler set out for Caracas by steamer in early May.[26]

Soon after, he began to send entries from his journal to London for publication. "May 23.—Today I had an interview with the minister for foreign affairs . . . I then saw the minister of the Interior to whom I proposed some questions. When he saw I had a predilection for the Barinas, he said he would introduce me to the representative of that province." It all looked promising, but nothing came of these meetings. Just as he did in Ohio, Etzler had trouble committing to an actual piece of earth. The savannas of the Barinas region sounded good—deep and fertile, he said, "but it would require much labour to keep back the weeds. In the wet season fevers prevail." He defined exact conditions for his settlement and would accept nothing less. It had to be "free of woods, level, capable of irrigation during the dry season, having no fearful swamps, nor any of such to the wind-ward, and within a day's journey from a navigable water in connection to the sea." In addition, it had to be high enough to have an average temperature of 77° Fahrenheit. He defined his way out of every opportunity. Later, he blamed the London directors for tying his hands, but in truth he had tied his own.

Nothing in Venezuela worked the way it was supposed to. News in August left Etzler stunned. The government did not keep records of lands occupied or sold, and they refused to promise that even if the colonists made considerable improvements, the state would sell them the land they occupied. Ministers and their representatives met with him and listened patiently, but he failed to move them. Given no choice but to seek title to land, with morale in England fading, the three agents made two purchases. In October, Carr and Taylor paid $550 (U.S. dollars, or so it appears) to a private owner for 120 acres on the southern shore of Paria, on a bay called Guinimita (latitude 10° 38' 48" north, longitude 62° 1' 6" west), located 36.5 miles west of Port of Spain. Etzler, then 400 miles away, near the city of Valencia, could not be consulted, so the agents acted without him. *The Morning Star* reported, "Descriptions of various estates were sent over by Taylor and Carr. Guinimita being the one which appeared to be the most eligible." The agents described most of the land as poor and hilly but "a sanitary locality for the members, being dry and breezy." They would prepare the high ground until the flatlands could be rid of mosquitoes by clearing and planting.[27] They knew nothing about the weather patterns of the site. Worse, they planned too much work in too little time, claiming that together they could clear enough brush and sow enough corn, pumpkins, rice, and peas to feed the pioneers. They imagined good fodder for animals, a chicken yard, fruit trees, and rows of vegetables for a thousand residents.

Etzler made his own deal. He toured possible properties with a Colonel Uslar, a German who had come to fight with the Republicans in their war of independence with Spain and had stayed on to become a kind of grandee. Uslar introduced Etzler to Fernando Bolívar, nephew of the liberator of Venezuela. Acting as real estate agents, Uslar and Bolívar showed Etzler various properties in the region, including an abandoned plantation where coffee and sugar had been grown some years before. There were buildings, ditches for irrigation, brick floors, banana trees in full bearing, and enough space to lodge 240 people. The directors in London had given Etzler instructions to seek a grant from the government and had only approved funds to be spent on Guinimita. (Explained the directors, "We had been expecting Mr. E. would have obtained a grant free of all cost. We therefore declined to follow his recommendation for the present, requesting him to return to Trinidad to assist our agents there.") Etzler disregarded their wishes, agreeing to pay $8,000 for the estate. (It isn't clear where he found the money.) The nearby planters, solicited by Uslar and Bolívar, put up $5,000 to reduce the price, probably calculating that their new neighbor would bring them some advantage. Etzler urged the directors in London to send members to his new estate, but they refused, choosing instead "to make our own property successful." The leadership seethed with resentment. An idealist who sought to unify humanity had acted alone. An inventor who asserted that any wilderness could be cultivated by his transforming machine had purchased an estate cleared and planted the old-fashioned way, possibly with slave labor. He apparently moved his family to the plantation and then set out to pursue various projects in the region.[28]

Land in Venezuela caused one kind of tension; the Satellite caused another. The society's scientific committee announced in April that a panel of engineers led by Thomas Atkins of Bicester would build an operating Satellite within ten weeks, by the middle of June. Stollmeyer knew something that no one else did—the machine under construction that spring was not the first of its kind. Etzler had tested a Satellite in 1843 at the Universal Peace Union in Butler County, Pennsylvania, months after meeting the strange and mystical Andrew Smolnikar, a former Benedictine monk who declared himself a prophet. Smolnikar told the story himself decades later. After reading about the Satellite, he found a mechanic who wagered "all his property as security, that he could put Etzler's machine in operation." Then came a portent. A woman described by Smolnikar as a "seeress who belonged to our association . . . received in a vision its whole structure." She dreamed the blueprint, dreamed it come to life, and dreamed that it splintered into a thousand pieces. For his part, Smolnikar had no love for Etzler, calling him a negative force in the world, even comparing him to Napoleon as one who set out "to subdue the world by physical means." The mad monk wanted a Satellite of his very own so he could "awaken nations from their materialism to our message of peace containing the true spiritualism." All that weirdness led to a cosmic setup, and Etzler walked right into it. He built his machine and watched it splinter into a thousand pieces.[29] There is no journalistic record of the event, and Etzler never mentioned it except to say that he would never again build a Satellite out of wood.

Finished in September, just as the first tantalizing news of Etzler's negotiations with the Venezuelan government came before the shareholders, the new Satellite carried the entire burden of the project and lumbered into its public trial with all the spooky expectation and mystical excitement of a séance. Stollmeyer placed placards around Oxfordshire to bring in a crowd. Concessionaires selling food showed up, creating the atmosphere of a country fair.[30] When it was over, everyone from the directors to the drunken revelers seemed unsure of what they had seen. The sporadically moving and squeaking contraption that bridled against its ropes and clawed at the ground forced them to make up their own minds about whether it did anything at all. Stollmeyer moved immediately to spin opinion. Within two hours he had convened a meeting of witnesses and forced through a hasty resolution: "Resolved—That the experiment with the Satellite and the connecting means has proved the practicability and applicability of both, and that the obstacles to its successful working are easily remediable." A specific controversy had to do with what he termed the "connecting means," or the method by which the Satellite attached to the cables that delivered its power. Some claimed that the engineer in charge did not build Etzler's design. "The fact is," wrote Stollmeyer the week after, "all the connecting means proposed by Mr. Etzler, namely, central drum, ropes, and levers, have been used." Why had the engineer ended the trial so abruptly, and earlier than expected? "Because all our members present with whom I could consult were satisfied with the trial."

Stollmeyer's efforts only fed the criticism. The *Banbury Guardian* gave the most unappealing account, saying that the events of that September day provided "no practical proof" that the Satellite would work; the system had not been built in its entirety—no reservoir, no windmills. They expressed disappointment when the thing fell so far short of its hoped-for "almost supernatural capabilities."[31] Stollmeyer fumed, but the membership shrugged it off. The Bradford branch laughed at the quibbling and toasted their imminent freedom with a "Satellite Ball," only briefly permitting a representative from London to interrupt the frivolity in order to read an official report in which Stollmeyer declared, "A mechanical triumph has been achieved by the aid and small contributions of working men."[32] They drank to Etzler's Satellite.

Could it have worked? With a little tweaking? With the

whole system in place? Not in a million years. Etzler grossly underestimated the loss of energy owing to friction. Ropes so long, running over rollers and turning around pivots, seeped away energy in the form of useless heat. The attrition would have rendered the power on the far end of the line insufficient to move such a large body. And like the Naval Automaton, the design assumed specific conditions (constant wind, shallow groundwater) that might not exist in Venezuela— yet another example of how nowhere and everywhere were the same for Etzler. Derisive criticism of the machine began months before the trial, when Stollmeyer fended off a ferocious attack published in *The New Moral World*, Robert Owen's journal. An anonymous engineer declared that a six-ton wagon with spiked wheels would sink into the muck. In addition, resistance from those spikes would be 14,000 pounds, and each rope would need to overcome 2,110 pounds of resistance—three times what Etzler had estimated.

It is tempting to think of Etzler as an innovator of clean, renewable energy systems, but that implies a sense of economy he never demonstrated. He made no attempt to think through an energy budget in estimating the work capacity of his machines. He neglected friction, not necessarily because he denied its reality, but because he was so smitten with the unending *supply* of energy that he never bothered to estimate it in units. How hard would the wind have to blow to turn the windmills? How high did the ocean swells need to rise in order to move the Naval Automaton at a given speed? What size engine would it take to move the floating island? In fact, no machine based on wind or water could have generated the power Etzler needed. And although his work might look like some Paleolithic version of industrial ecology—the science of reengineering production to function within ecological systems—that would also be too generous. Just as he never bothered with units of energy, he also never bothered with material units. Etzler had no need for efficiency, for he recognized nothing that needed to be conserved.

The Satellite is a metaphor for economic growth. Its inventor thought only of the mechanism and not a whit about the land that made its operation economical. He regarded the only limiting factor to be technical form, without in any way allowing for limitations in natural capital or energy. In this, Etzler was no different from other believers in material progress from his time to our own. Growth has existed in the historical moment that he shares with Adam Smith, Alexander Hamilton, W. W. Rostow, and Alan Greenspan, a moment during which matter in usable form—what we call resources—could be viewed as limited only by its cost.[33]

Stollmeyer replied to every attack, not allowing any doubt to linger lest it be accepted as fact. But it is clear that if Etzler himself had constructed the complete system and given the word, the water would have poured over the spillway and hit the wheel . . . and nothing else would have happened. The ropes would have tugged against the hapless frame. Whether he or Stollmeyer admitted that possibility even to themselves is impossible to know. Some things lie too deep for tears. In the meantime, the tropics began to look like their Plan B. The Satellite remained crucial to the morale of the society, but the Torrid Zone suggested a kind of *machine itself*, a geographical manifestation of the same energy they hoped to focus through the Satellite.

•

A year had passed since the first meeting at Etzler's home in London, and the ever-defensive Stollmeyer—self-appointed minister of information—listed the Tropical Emigration Society's accomplishments. Distributed shares came to 2,148 in the hands of 1,557 subscribers, representing approximately 7,000 family members. A month later, subscriptions had doubled to 5,000 shares, representing perhaps as many as 17,000 people. The society existed in thirty-six cities, with eight branches in London alone. The leadership called a tea for the pioneers before their imminent departure, declaring "a day of rejoicing throughout the whole Society." Stoll-meyer, blocking out all the background noise, declared again that the society possessed a working Satellite, termed an "iron slave, which in its multiplication will break the chains of human slaves by superceding them." They had money in the bank (about £650), a steam engine, and a soon-to-be colony in Venezuela. Word arrived from Carr and Taylor that they had identified the peninsula of Paria as a promising site for a temporary settlement. The fifty pioneers would live there, waiting for Etzler to finalize the location of the main settle-ment, at which time a larger group of volunteers would take possession of it.

To mark the occasion and the progress of a year's time, three hundred members met for a grand celebration. They toasted a glorious future, these mechanics and clerks, longing for something great in their lifetimes. Thomas Marshall, the bookseller from the East End who later shipped for South America, addressed the gathered with the hope that "people of all climates and of all countries, the source of all power,— may they soon be aroused from their lethargy and soon ob-tain possession of their rights, in order to erase from the pages of future history all distinctions of sect, class or party, that mankind may become one happy family of brothers, of friends, having one common interest,—the welfare and hap-piness of each other." Another wished that the society would "increase in numbers . . . to be a guiding star to the working and oppressed classes of those countries where the soil is monopolized, and where the institutions make the rich richer."[34]

The organization grew so numerous so quickly that some worried whether one settlement would be sufficient, so a Second Tropical Emigration Society started up "as assistance," to follow "immediately in its wake." Its founder and secretary would be Marshall. Yet things fell apart from the inside as circumstances began to press relentlessly against staggering presumptions. Members from the distant and suburban branches decried a lack of democratic process, saying that the London branch made all the decisions and generally snubbed them. Etzler's negotiations showed no results a year after he began them, and his purchase of the plantation near Valencia needed explaining. Worse, those who never accepted the Satellite as a functioning machine, after grumbling for months, took action. They referred to an earlier statement by the organization that should the Satellite fail to work as expected, "all engagements" between the society and its two principal leaders "shall cease." Tired of defending himself and Etzler against increasingly entrenched critics, Stollmeyer determined to kill every doubt by demonstrating success where it counted, in Venezuela. He sailed for Trinidad in November of 1845.

Captain Taylor was the first to die. He survived for thirteen agonizing days with an illness that Carr blamed on "drinking the water of four coco-nuts when extremely heated and over fatigued." Carr boated him to Port of Spain to find a doctor, but nothing could be done. Taylor perished two days later. The true killers might have been waterborne disease, malaria, or respiratory infection following exhaustion. Malnutrition would have made any sickness life threatening. With his coconut theory, Carr managed to blame the tropics and Taylor at the same time, making it possible for the folks back home to assimilate the death of one of their principle agents without sinking into doubt about the whole enterprise. It was a strategy Stollmeyer learned to imitate. Sensing the danger to morale, Carr cut short the mourning and took attention away from his fallen friend by announcing in the same letter that the ship carrying the pioneers had arrived in Trinidad.

Carr welcomed the millwrights, metalsmiths, and gardeners at Port of Spain, but the goodwill fell apart immediately.[35] The strangeness of the place, the heat of the day, the expectations hanging over them—all made them wither. They were only a few workers, with modest tools and no steady source of food. Supplies would come from Stollmeyer once he arrived in Trinidad, a lifeline that would make them dependent on him for survival should things go wrong. The pioneers also expected to make their way to the plantation Etzler had purchased near Valencia, thinking this was the permanent settlement. Carr broke the news to them—they weren't going to Valencia. First, the land belonged to Etzler, and the directors did not want members settling there. Second, Carr had no money to pay for their transportation anyway. He then ordered the carpenters and smiths to accompany him to Guinimita the next day. They refused. The pioneers did not recognize Carr's authority, considering themselves his equals, not his servants. They demanded to be included in every decision. The stalemate sat for a few days, until Stollmeyer landed and quickly met with the anxious and inflamed artisans. They finally agreed to a chain of command, with Carr in charge, and moved out to the peninsula.

With the pioneers slashing at the forest and eating salt pork, Etzler joined Stollmeyer at Port of Spain in early January 1846, but rather than work to ensure the stability of the preliminary settlement, they began building a floating island.

Stollmeyer recorded their plan in *The Morning Star*. They would construct a series of floats 13 feet long, 13 inches wide, and 6 inches high, made from bamboo and balsa wood. These would be strapped together in multiple layers until they formed a structure 144 feet long, 12 feet wide, and 5 or 6 feet thick. Their intent was to pilot the thing—more a raft than an island—to Guinimita, where the pioneers would help to increase its area still further. Stollmeyer estimated that the first section would contain houses and gardens. "As our means increase, more can easily be added and the whole combined . . . to go on the high sea." But Stollmeyer needed cash. He tried to goad the directors back in England into writing a check, but they rebuffed him. The labor of construction continued, but there was a general atmosphere of anxiety. If the floating island failed, they would have nothing to show for Etzler's system. The pioneers would then know that they had moved to Venezuela to expend their own energy, fend for themselves, and risk tropical disease, exhaustion, and death. Stollmeyer concluded his letter to the membership defiantly: check or no, "a float on a large scale *shall be* commenced." He recommitted himself to finishing the island in time to pilot it to England, where it would pick up the next company of subscribers for glorious transportation to Guinimita.[36]

Idealism smashed against biological reality. Sand flies bit the pioneers while they worked, and mosquitoes bit their faces at night. Rations ran low, so everyone cut back. None had ever lived without shelter under a burning sun. Some found refuge in a beached schooner near the marsh, but the boat became their coffin—a ferment of disease and sickness. Order broke down amid the fear and exhaustion. The men refused to work, refused orders, drank the liquor in their supplies, and screamed in the heat. After two weeks, stress and near starvation engulfed them. Carr stumbled into Port of Spain with two men, Dawson and Tucker, looking for supplies. Tucker had been working twelve to fourteen hours a day to build his own boat, and he was fading. The rum and toddy meant as a curative caused him to plummet. A doctor in Trinidad "blistered and purged the life out of him in two days." He was buried by his wife and four children. Carr showed up too sick to function, apparently suffering from "overexertion and anxiety of mind." Another boat arrived with the report that a Mr. Whitchurch had died, leaving a wife and three children at Guinimita.

Stollmeyer should have accepted these deaths as a sign of imminent disaster. He could have called all the pioneers to Port of Spain, restored and reprovisioned them, and rethought the mission. Instead, desperate for any excuse that would rescue the delusion he inhabited, he lashed out at the victims. "I can trace every case of sickness to individual or collective imprudence. The climate is certainly not to blame," he declared. Then, switching into the language of collateral damage, he continued: "Every battle costs many lives—the factories and coal mines have their victims—how then can we expect that an industrial army, composed of such materials, where selfishness reigns supreme, can escape uninjured. Onward we must look and not back, or we shall be turned into pillars of salt." With this appalling misplacement of ends and means, Stollmeyer did more to destroy the mission than anyone else. The weary industrial army—the same workingmen and -women whom he once celebrated for building a society dedicated to freedom and plenty—now became his excuse for a failed settlement.[37]

The membership in England, already committed to their course, seemed to have accepted Stollmeyer's version of events, and they cheered the departure of friends and family to Venezuela. They held teas and dances and composed songs as 92 men, 39 women, and 62 children (193 volunteers, not including infants) boarded the *Condor* for Guinimita on March 13, 1846. Thomas Marshall traveled with his young son, Arthur, in the tight quarters under the deck. Also on board was the tough-minded secretary, Thomas Powell, a bookkeeper and early leader in the society who realized that he would need to whip the ill-prepared and grasping colonists into a group that might be capable of surviving. A few days out, off the Isle of Wight, they all suffered seasickness, vomiting until they lay in a stupor. The passengers, whether from laziness or faintness, refused to prepare meals, then fought like alley cats over every scrap. For a week, "each meal became a scramble for a portion of food and of course the weakest obtained least." Powell stepped up to impose discipline and complained in print that an enlightened federation dedicated to eliminating greed and competition now depended on his pathetic crew of complaining shirkers. The company slowly recovered under his direction—surviving the horse latitudes and the birth of two children. Then, at ten o'clock on the morning of April 29, after laying off the coast for a day searching for life, the captain spotted a red flag flying from the top of a hill. The boat anchored, and everyone watched from the deck as Thomas Carr, accompanied by four local men, rowed out against the wind and whitecaps of the gulf.

They devoured fresh fruit in silence as Carr recited a slow and unaffected accounting of the dead: Mrs. Whitchurch and one of her three children, along with Amos Spencer and Messrs. Wood, White, Scholefield, Wilkinson, Samuel, Craddock, Burden, Ford, and Miss Handby, along with Mr. Whitchurch, Tucker, and Taylor. In total, fifteen of the forty-one pioneers succumbed in less than five months. In the two weeks leading up to the final abandonment of the settlement, the survivors had nothing to eat but flour and water. Now Carr wanted this fresh crew to follow him back to Guinimita to stoop over the graves of their friends and neighbors. The volunteers looked out into the hot wind, across the bay to the glare reflecting off the sand, to the prickly brush that covered the hills, to the narrow valleys—land that needed bodily labor to make it livable. Carr finally told them the truth. The swamp had not been cleared. Most everyone associated marshes with disease, so the continued existence of standing water so far into the year signaled failure and futility. "Nearly twenty acres of land was ready to be sown, or set with food for our sustenance, which could be ripe in three months," reported Powell, but that meant nothing had been planted during the previous six months. They would live off of supplies from Port of Spain—flour and water. They would have to walk a mile every day to fill their buckets at a spring. Even more outrageous, only a single house had been completed.[38]

This bleak confession emboldened a group who had become discouraged while at sea. They called a meeting. Powell stood aside while his broken ranks deliberated. The meeting ended with a short resolution. They would ask Etzler and Stollmeyer what to do next, "seeing that this preliminary settlement was unhealthy, and had been abandoned by the volunteers and pioneers." Some wanted to find a new location. Forty-five people argued in favor of going ashore at Guinimita, thinking that "with prudence and perseverance, the plans of the Society would be . . . carried out." The greatest number, 148, refused to leave the *Condor* and verbally attacked Carr, screaming abuse at him for not writing sooner with what he knew. Several threatened to kill him. Carr tore himself free from the ship, but by the time he did, they had arrived at Port of Spain. Everyone assumed that Etzler would come aboard and set things right, but just the day before, anticipating the arrival of the volunteers, he took off for British Guiana. Even Stollmeyer could not explain why. "I expect," sneered Powell, "his journey is more on his own account than for our society." They peppered Stollmeyer with questions when he came aboard. He offered to find them a small plot of land in Trinidad as a new preliminary settlement. But the objectors—worn out by the voyage, terrified of death, and livid—demanded that the society pay their passage to England or the United States. Powell promised that he would see them cross to safety. He went from ship to shore and back for more than two days, negotiating with a despondent Carr for £500, finally squeezing out of him £450 in unauthorized funds. The *Condor* sailed for New Orleans the following morning.[39]

Meanwhile, the government of Trinidad had taken notice of the debacle. Sir Henry Macleod, colonial governor, appointed a committee to inquire into "certain immigrants who arrived in this colony on the 3rd of December last . . . and also into the cause of the numerous deaths that had since occurred." It looked like a police investigation and ended in a public meeting. The report concluded that "never, probably, did any body of European immigrants, since Europeans first became immigrants to the tropical climates, find themselves in such a state of destitution and unmitigated misery as these unfortunate beings during their brief location at Guinimita." They held Stollmeyer personally accountable and, short of charging him with any crime, publicly accused him of "cold-blooded brutality of expression" in the way he condemned the victims. The committee called the settlement "this system of murder [that] cannot be suffered to last any longer."[40] Macleod's report provides third-party objectivity. People outside the cloud that hung over Stollmeyer saw the madness of the project.

Powell publicly denounced Etzler in his next letter, written in May. "Mr. E may be an inventor, a genius, if it will please anyone, but he is not a practical man; he cannot carry out his own measures; he lacks the energy necessary to set his own machines going." If the society really wanted to enact his plan, they needed people of "less pretension to talent to perform the task." Etzler explained his actions in a letter dated before Powell's and postmarked Georgetown, British Guiana. He tossed light regret at the defection of the *Condor*: "It will now take some time for recovering from the shock of disappointment." Since the leadership no longer appreciated him, he decided to find people who would. He accepted an invitation from the government of British Guiana. With that, he walked away. "I have now, individually, to struggle on in the wilderness." Later, *The Morning Star* reported that Etzler had turned up as engineering director of a railway project in Trinidad, but he never actually joined the business, at least not for very long. In his last missive he announced, "I am going to the United States." Etzler satisfied himself that he had left detailed advice in Trinidad for those who had survived Guinimita, "which advice expressed also my anticipation of their total disappointment, and what they might possibly do for themselves." He accepted no responsibility, leaving them empty, telling them of their good fortune to find themselves "in a beautiful country, where labour is so much wanted, and nature requires so little."[41]

Without so much as a gesture to those who gave their lives under his promises, who put their money and hopes in him when they had nothing, and without admitting his own complicity in the disaster, Etzler vanished in July or August of 1846. It would be left for Stollmeyer to hear the last from him and speculate about the whereabouts of the visionary, his wife, and her family.

The exit of the philosophical leader did not cause the collapse of the Tropical Emigration Society. Etzler and Stollmeyer had always set themselves apart from the membership, never bothering with the details of colonization. Though they urged and inspired the entire misadventure, they disavowed the outcome. They enjoyed special provisions (such as the one giving them free shares in recognition of the resources they brought), but never fully associated themselves with the colony. Etzler's abandonment meant little to the project, which had never benefited from his inventions anyway. Powell kept discipline through the summer of 1846 to make the settlement in Trinidad (known as the Erthig Estate) stable, and he conducted the sale of Guinimita. The inhabitants finally found consensus and did their field labor without world-transforming machines. They subsisted on what food they could grow and on small wages earned in town. Many of them never left Trinidad, but ten refused to give up the dream of an exemplary settlement. In August the Second Tropical Emigration Society purchased a place known as La Union, on a "little known and seldom visited" stretch of river that emptied into the Gulf of Paria. It took three days for the settlers to reach it. Even *The Morning Star* came to its senses and dissuaded them, describing them as "a few zealots." Since they had no way to post a letter, all communication with them ceased.

In November, Powell sailed to La Union to deliver supplies. On the way, he put in at the town of Guiria and spent a few days looking around. Nearby, he came to a small house and the remains of a six-acre garden. Cucumbers, tomatoes, melons, and other fruits grew wild. The ground was flat, with a river at one side and the bay to the south. "It would have been the very place for our preliminary settlement," he wrote. "Every inch might have been worked by the Satellite." But it was too late. "Our money has been expended, and our members' lives sacrificed uselessly, without the slightest bene-fit." Days later, Powell and the crew of his small boat fired their guns at the mouth of the river to announce their arrival at La Union. A mile upstream, along narrow banks, slashing through vines and branches to make their way, they found the colony. The men grew sugarcane, rice, maize, and plan-tains, but they lived mostly on wild pigs, bananas, coffee, and bread made from cassava. Powell brought them heavy stores—shot and powder, five hundred feet of cut boards, pants and soap, flour, two barrels of biscuits, hams, cheese, cutlasses, hatchets, and hammers. He slept the night in a small cabin.

At sunrise they led him to the grave of Thomas Marshall. Marshall had watched the *Condor* sail away and never let go of the ideals of the society. He wrote this from Trinidad: "All I say is—the Tropics forever . . . My return will not be looked for so long as there is half a chance left."[42] Powell recorded the few details: "His remains are laid in a quiet and unobtru-sive spot. He caught cold on his way to La Union, and could not recover the injury." Marshall had died on October 16, leaving his son. Powell never returned. The La Union colony starved on its dwindling supplies and what little its members could grow. The last word from the settlement said that their corn harvest had nearly failed. The London directors could no longer sustain them, and they lost contact. In the final edition of *The Morning Star*, one member mourned La Union with a sense of reality never heard in the early days of the Venezuela mission: "They have inefficient shelter—are short of food. The place is hot, and damp, and confined, whilst the men have scarce either protection or provisions.

What was to have been anticipated? What else but that which arrived—fevers, agues, and death!" La Union retreated into memory without further news of its condition, like a boat un-knotted from its mooring, drifting into fog. No one ever heard from its inhabitants again.

With the membership evaporated, only the London meet-ing of the Tropical Emigration Society continued. The weirdly implacable ones spoke with buttoned-up dignity to a frigid, empty room. They voted to alter the constitution to allow a quorum of five members rather than nine so that they could pass binding resolutions—with no one and nothing to bind. News of the society continued for a time in *The Re-former*, but later that year, the London meeting disbanded.[43]

•

The disaster in Venezuela cannot be reduced to a parable. The psychology of those involved and the power relations be-tween the leadership and the men on the ground certainly contributed to the outcome. Yet the project unfolded under a spell much larger than Etzler could have cast. Anyone reading political economy in the 1840s came across such dubious statements as "The productive energies of the material world, are always equal to the supply of human wants."[44] Many shared in the belief that accumulation accorded with the un-derlying logic of the universe, that human wants joined in the natural order.[45] Another paradox of Western thought at the end of the Enlightenment was that although it insisted on the unity of nature and society, that unity never existed at the level of biology. The ideal of human progress never formed a parallel between the merchant's economy and the economy of living things.

All this seems a long way from the dead at Guinimita, but it isn't. Ideas influence behavior, especially among those who claim to live by philosophy. Stollmeyer's hesitation to provide adequate supplies, and Etzler's preoccupation with the float-ing island—and not with the sick and starving just a day's voyage away—stemmed from their insistence that nature guaranteed human betterment. Stollmeyer blamed the vic-tims rather than admit that nature does not labor for any-one's benefit. Etzler skipped out because staying to manage the crisis would have forced him into practicality, logistics, compromise. Rather than rethink their idealism, the partners clung to it because it told them things about the moral and material world that they desperately wanted to believe.

•

John Roebling designed the first wire-rope suspension bridge in 1845. Still living at Saxonburg, he entered a competition for an aqueduct over the Allegheny River. The 162-foot span carried the flow of the Pennsylvania Main Line Canal into downtown Pittsburgh, using white pine for its major beams and two hundred thousand pounds of wire bundled together. He built a highway bridge in the same year, and then in 1848 he moved his manufacturing operation to Tren-ton, New Jersey. In the winter of 1852, Roebling found himself stranded on a boat caught in an ice floe while cross-ing the East River. The experience made him think about a bridge. Four years later he was at work on a multi-span to link Manhattan and Brooklyn. Masonry towers, their founda-tions deep in the riverbed, supported cables anchored at each end. Vertical rods connected the roadway to the cables. Roebling's wire rope held the entire weight. The structure formed a truss, with the cables in constant tension and the towers in constant compression. As Alan Trachtenberg put it, "Viewed theoretically, the structure was a unity of oppo-site forces."[46] During construction of the Brooklyn Bridge, in

1869, a ferry coming in to dock crushed Roebling's foot. Infection killed him two weeks later. Just like Etzler, he managed to fuse idealism and materialism, philosophy and engineering in everything he attempted, writing in 1864, "When I am . . . endeavoring to carry out my conception practically and materially for the actual welfare of my fellowmen, then I am also living a useful natural life."[47]

Conrad Stollmeyer did his final service to the Tropical Emigration Society by aiding the settlers as they trickled into Port of Spain. He saw Etzler for the last time in 1846 and decided to stay in Trinidad. Looking around, he saw opportunities to improve the island everywhere. He collected manure from some source—possibly human—to compete with the bird guano being mined off the coast of Peru. He bought and sold scrap metal and exported it (iron, copper, lead, brass, pewter) to the United States. He constructed a water main for Port of Spain by contract with the city. He bought a three-hundred-acre estate near the Pitch Lake, a kind of petroleum seep, and served as local agent for the tenth Earl of Dundonald (Thomas Cochrane) during the earl's service to the Royal Navy as commander of the West Indies station. Stollmeyer died on April 30, 1904, two years after a fire destroyed his home and private papers. His son, Charles Fourier Stollmeyer, built an oddball castle in the center of town (known as Stollmeyer's Castle) designed by a Scottish architect to resemble Balmoral. Two of Conrad's great-grandsons were Victor and Jeffery Stollmeyer, both formidable right-handed batsmen. Jeffery had a leg-break googly and played thirty-two tests in his career as a cricketer for Trinidad.

Etzler did not return to the United States. If he had, he would have surfaced somewhere, published something, and pursued some other project. But there is nothing. In 1853 Stollmeyer wrote to an old friend from Philadelphia, Samuel

S. Rex, "I have never heard a word of the whereabouts of Mr. Etzler. I thought the great exhibition in London or New York would fetch him to either of those places, but could never learn whether he is amongst the living or the dead." Rex reported that he had not seen Etzler since 1840. In another letter to Rex, dated January 25, 1854, Stollmeyer mentioned that Etzler had left from the beach at La Guaira, near Caracas, for the island of Curaçao, 170 miles away by sea, but Stollmeyer was "unable to say whether he ever arrived at Curaçao or what has become of him." In 1855 he wrote to another acquaintance: "I have not heard anything from Mr. Etzler since he left Venezuela about 8 years ago." It is not likely that Etzler lived in obscurity, never making another noise.[48] What follows is the most probable ending.

The family secured a small boat on the beach, but none of them knew the tides or winds, and though Etzler had crossed the Atlantic six or eight times, he didn't know how to sail. They headed northwest into the Caribbean. The trade winds coming from out of the northeast would have continually sent them toward shore while they strained to make headway through white-capped swells five or six feet high. Even if they had seen the tiny coral island—a speck in the blue even at close distance—it might not have helped them. They would have needed to know the location of Curaçao long before they saw it. They missed it and its narrow port at Willemstad and slipped between Aruba and the Paraguaná peninsula, blown clear of land and into the open sea toward Mexico, burned and crying into the waves and the interminable wind. Inundated, they went over. The sun and tides surrounded them now; all distinctions vanished. They prayed to forces they once held in their hands as their own heat dissipated into the entropic universe.

CHAPTER FOUR

Seven Billion Billionaires

I t is proved and it did not happen." That is how the historian and journalist Bernard De Voto described Etzler's plan for paradise in *Harper's* magazine in 1936. It did not happen, said De Voto, because Etzler extrapolated from what little he knew (precariously); his mathematics allowed for nothing unforeseen (catastrophically); and he believed that reason always triumphed (naively). "Etzler's vision," said De Voto, "came down to a promise that man's will would yet be law to the physical world." Time and again, Etzler imagined principles that had no relation to any particular environment or set of conditions, an error he acquired from one of the major misconceptions of his time—mechanism, or the idea that universal laws of motion and force superseded organic nature. In another sense, it *did* happen. Etzler's paradise came down to a realm of pleasure and convenience strikingly similar to the highway-strip, big-box-store, low-rise-condo sprawl that has caused so many people to reconsider the meaning of consumption. Etzler accurately predicted in the 1830s that people would turn their minds "to the earthly improvements of life," that they would increasingly define their well-being by their standard of living. Future boosters of economic growth would speak the same language of transformation, harmony, and wealth.[1]

The dream of progress in the nineteenth century held that nature never resisted or contradicted human wants. And though no one else stated things exactly as Etzler did, the notion that nature has a distinctly human purpose has had a long career. Consider another futurist, R. Buckminster Fuller. Kicked out of Harvard for extravagance and unfitting behavior, Fuller worked as a meat-packer. He married and started a business but went bankrupt in 1927, just at the time that his daughter Alexandra fell ill and died. Tormented by guilt that he had failed to provide her with living conditions basic to human health, Fuller dedicated the rest of his life to innovations that made the most of available resources, toward a greater material stability for every member of society. Turning to his childhood love of building and the technical skills he acquired while a naval radio operator during World War I, he invented the 4D House (later called the Dymaxion House), a model for efficient living.

For the reborn Fuller, improving the world meant redesigning it. A decade later he published his first book, *Nine Chains to the Moon* (1938), employing an I-have-seen-the-future language that might have come right out of Etzler's *Paradise*. Fuller announced, "Industrial changes greater than any in history are at hand. The duration of the period of transition will be variable in direct proportion to the intelligence and support given to advancing industry." It's a big universe, he chided readers, so enlarge your sense of the possible to equal it.[2]

Fuller was the Etzler of the 1930s. And just as Etzler began with architecture, Fuller's journey began with the house. The house is the physical space where subsistence practices and the environment produce culture—where wheat becomes bread, wood becomes tools, and biological reproduction becomes social reproduction. Fuller understood that a big chunk of everything consumed by people passes through the domicile. A new design would not only increase resource efficiency, it would serve as a stamping mill for a new twentieth-century human—or, as he said, "The goal is the emergence of humanity." In the houses Fuller imagined, people would be freer—"free to explore, free to devise, include, refine, free to compose and synchronize."[3] He didn't stop with the house. The Dymaxion Car had a teardrop shape and operated on three wheels. He conceived of a submarine island anchored to the bottom of the ocean, with a periscope-like pipe for air and radio communication. Then there were the many shapes and structures, some actually constructed (such as the geodesic dome). All his inventions had the same premise—that new spaces created new social potential by connecting people to one another and to the universe in new ways.

Economic growth lay implicitly within Fuller's optimism, taking the form of the dividend earned from design according to cosmic principles. But he had a problem. Resources looked to be in short supply (or just too expensive) during the worst depression in American history. While searching for a way to create growth without added material, he hit upon the idea that matter cost money but that, eventually, energy would not. His solution: there would be an "ephemeralization" of society. He meant that increasing units of increasingly available and inexpensive energy would create a rapid circulation of matter, such that its forms would be short-lived. Fuller saw energy replacing matter in all but the basic necessities. Electricity, in particular, looked to be proliferating: "Industrial research is now working in 70 bands of energy radiation . . . This is proof-positive of a mind-over-matter dominance and frees mind-over-matter dominance from a purely 'mystical' or 'literary' connotation into a bread-and-butter economic significance . . . EFFICIENCY EPHEMERALIZES."[4] Like Hegel, Fuller saw a parallel between mind and universe. Like Etzler, he bet everything on an open-ended source of power. His influences might have been different, but his idealism is strikingly similar. Fuller told his Depression-weary readers that they would soon be free of scarcity: "The quantity of physical, cosmic energy . . . arriving aboard planet Earth each minute is greater than all the energy used annually by all humanity . . . We have four billion billionaires aboard our planet, as accounted by *real wealth*."[5]

Fuller walked in a familiar groove, using physics to bypass the social and political institutions that actually made up the economy. Recall that in the 1840s, social thinkers of all kinds, blown away by the explanatory power of Newton's bodies in motion, argued that laws akin to gravity regulated the economic motion currency and cotton. By the 1870s, economic thought had fallen into a murky place. The very people who should have been most capable of observing the actual stock of resources became blind to the effects of economic and territorial expansion. Under systematic hunting, bison plummeted from fifteen million animals in 1865 (some put the original number as high as twenty-five million) to near extinction by 1885. Passenger pigeons went the same way, once numbering as many as five billion individuals, comprising 40 percent of all the birds in North America, but nearly extinct by 1879 (extinct by 1914). The Schuylkill River in Philadelphia, along with rivers throughout New York and New England, stank with the runoff of human sewage and the chemical waste pouring in from hundreds of factories. Then, in 1865, the USDA warned the public of a "permanent national famine of wood." Others wrote that the rising demand for forest trees would make wood too scarce to satisfy even "the ordinary necessities of life."[6] Lots of things once thought to be as immeasurable as the sky seemed to be crashing.

The "timber famine" should have caught everyone's attention. What could have been more important than wood? Congress acted by passing the Timber Culture Act of 1873, followed by the Forest Reserve Act of 1891, and it decried "the senseless devastation of the forests in the United States."[7] Yet Amasa Walker, David A. Wells, Simon Newcomb, Henry C. Carey, and William Graham Sumner—the major political economists writing at the time—made no comment. An observer of the lumber industry wrote in 1876 that "the greatest and most shameful waste of this indispensable material has become the order of the day, while our Boards of Trade, our political economists and statesmen, and the leading journals of the country, totally ignore the subject."[8] This odd inability to recognize what others noted with alarm affected the way political economists calculated wealth, advised governments, and influenced the public, and it played a role in the emergence of professional economics. But why did the most ardent materialist thinkers ignore changes in the material world? Some idea or habit of mind prevented them from seeing the economy as part of the environment. That thing was physics.

Social theorists of the eighteenth and nineteenth centuries had little use for the organism as a metaphor. It followed an inexorable cycle—birth, death, and disintegration. Its vital force came from *within* rather than from *without*, strangely evoking the soul, an inscrutable entity beyond empirical investigation. Life revealed no laws, so it yielded no theory. Medieval metaphors also did not lend themselves to a world in the flux of proliferating knowledge. They tended to emphasize the authority of heaven. The Great Chain of Being depicted God on top, rocks on the bottom, and every human, animal, and plant organized into eternal ranks. The plentitude, continuity, and eternalness of the Great Chain of Being gained in popularity into the eighteenth century as philosophers and poets embraced it. But beginning in the seventeenth century, scientific thinkers bridled under its inherent mysticism. They increasingly rejected it in favor of a metaphor that conformed better to things they had learned by experience. Mechanism did away with hierarchies and mysteries. It proclaimed that life was conceived of as made of discrete parts and governed by measurable forces. Newton's cosmos could be explained mathematically; its variables could be manipulated and its principles applied everywhere. In this way, physics not only named the cards but the rules of the game. It offered an internally consistent thought chamber where things worked predictably. Fascination with it as a template for society increased during the second half of the eighteenth century because rather than celebrate plentitude, mechanism simplified complexity.[9]

Take for example the atom. Long before anyone had actually seen or detected protons and neutrons surrounded by an electron cloud, the atom was a hypothetical body: the basic unit of all matter, something so small that it could not be divided into anything else. The English word dates to 1477. Political economists saw a similarity between the *individual* (something *indivisible*; the word started out in 1425) and the atom. Both could be understood as the basic constituents of much larger systems. (*Individual* found its modern meaning in the seventeenth century, describing not just a person but a separate and distinct person.) But where would anyone have seen people behaving as atoms? People still defined themselves by their membership in families, towns, and parishes. No one really worked or worshiped as an individual. A physics of society must have been born in the marketplace. Think of a busy city square, with buyers moving from cart to cart making exchanges with sellers. To eighteenth- and nineteenth-century observers, no collective metaphor fitted the picture. Every person appeared to act for himself, dealing to serve his own needs. Looking at the market as the epitome of social life—ignoring households, guilds, or any of the other commonplace collectives that would have muddied the waters of pure theory—it appeared as thousands of particles doing exactly the same thing. After all, buyers and sellers did not act randomly; they followed certain conventions, certain rules. Adam Smith saw social atoms moving according to some unseen force that transcended the history and institutions of society itself.

Economists seized upon physics without understanding the full implication of the categories they clumsily translated into human action. It is more than just curious that so many political economists studied the sciences. David Wells published *Principles and Applications of Chemistry* (1858) and other similar books while he taught agricultural chemistry. He went on to become one of the most talented economists in the U.S. federal government. Simon Newcomb authored papers on the transit of Venus and the orbits of Neptune and Uranus throughout the 1870s as an astronomer for the United States Navy. He published his *Principles of Political Economy* in 1885. Erasmus Peshine Smith, a protégé of Henry Carey's, announced, in his *Manual of Political Economy* (1853), "The writer has made the attempt to construct a skeleton of Political economy upon the basis of purely physical laws." According to the Irish economist John Cairnes, "Political Economy plainly belongs to the same class of sciences with mechanics, astronomy, optics, chemistry, electricity, and, in general, all those physical sciences which have reached the inductive stage." Amasa Walker published *The*

Science of Wealth (1866), in which he asserted, "So far as political economy, as a science, is physical, depending on the forces and agencies of nature, it is above legislation," meaning that its truths could no more be shaped by human will than could gravitation.[10]

The most notable of this group was Henry Carey. He grew up in the publishing house of his father, the Revolutionary printer and industrial booster Mathew Carey, and began writing about economy during the 1830s. Carey advised Abraham Lincoln during the Civil War, wrote ten books and hundreds of articles (most of them as a columnist for Horace Greeley's *New York Tribune*), and influenced a generation of business leaders. Marx regarded him as the only American worth citing; Ralph Waldo Emerson quoted and celebrated him in his essay "Farming"; John Stuart Mill argued with him; and every Republican treasury secretary after the Civil War visited his Philadelphia salon. The Wharton School at the University of Pennsylvania was founded to perpetuate his ideas. Though almost forgotten today, Carey was the most visible, influential, and imaginative political economist in the United States for three decades.[11]

Carey embraced the conservation of matter (not to be confused with the first law of thermodynamics, the conservation of energy). He imagined the economy as a great cosmic cycle. "Man," he wrote, "can neither create nor destroy a particle of matter, nor can he affect the quantity of force in the world. His power is limited to altering the mode of its manifestation." Once matter moves through the economy, ending up as empty bottles, chicken bones, and scrap metal, thought Carey, it "enters into a new equilibrium with one or more of the liberated forces, to remain at rest until again evoked for fresh labor . . . We have here perpetual circulation."[12] Everything cycled around, so nothing ran out. Since

scarcity did not exist in the universe, said Carey, it did not exist in human societies either. But a little physics is a dangerous thing. Carey had this much right—matter in the universe
is conserved. It cannot be consumed out of existence. But
that fact has no economic consequence. The conservation of
matter has nothing to say about the relative abundance or
scarcity of matter in *particular forms*—such as bison and
trees. Sure they're made of elements, but what good are elements? In the transformation of matter, wrote the chemist
John Pitkin Norton, "we discover that *nothing is lost*: if we
burn a piece of wood it disappears, but has merely been converted into carbonic acid and water." But something is lost.
The wood! By substituting physics for biology, Carey failed
to see organisms and thus environments.[13]

It is unfortunate that Carey never debated one of his
most insightful contemporaries, George Perkins Marsh. While
Carey considered every incursion into the forest a sign of
increasing order and harmony in the world, Marsh had a
more sober view. Without romanticism or idealism, and without reference to political economy at all, this scholar and
politician from Vermont expressed a contrary vision of human progress—researched and argued with encyclopedic detail in *Man and Nature, or, Physical Geography as Modified by
Human Action* (1864). Marsh believed that moving from
barbarism to civilization inevitably heightened the conflict
between people and their environments, that attaining
modernity meant attaining the technological power and the
force of numbers to do real damage. He presented his own
theory of stages, only his story does not turn out very well for
civil society. People multiplied; filled the riverbanks, the
meadows, and the coastlines; then realized that they could
find more "room for expansion and further growth" only by
removing the forests. That historical moment meant some-

thing profound to Marsh: "The destruction of the woods, then, was man's first physical conquest, his first violation of the harmonies of inanimate nature." He worried about the collapse of his civilization under rampant deforestation and soil erosion—effects he himself had witnessed in New England's rocketing economic development. But if there is one passage that expresses his ambivalence toward progress, it might be this one: "Every human movement, every organic act, every volition . . . is accompanied with atomic disturbance, and hence every such movement, every such act or process affects all the atoms of universal matter." The interconnectedness of all things implies the very feedback that advocates of growth denied at all costs.[14]

One law is conspicuously missing from Carey's thought: the second law of thermodynamics—the supreme economic law of the universe. Carey never mentioned it, though he knew about it through one of its most brilliant interpreters—John Tyndall. Tyndall's *Heat Considered as a Mode of Motion* (1863) is quoted in Carey's *Manual of Social Science* (1872), in which Tyndall speaks of the first law and the many forms that energy takes. In the same work, Tyndall states the second law with striking clarity: "For every stroke of work done by the steam-engine, for every pound that it lifts, and for every wheel that it sets in motion, an equivalent of heat disappears."[15] Carey also cited perhaps the most widely read work on the subject, *The Correlation and Conservation of Forces* (1865), a series of essays edited by Edward L. Youmans, author of many popular works of science. The gravitas of the book comes from a lecture by Hermann Ludwig Ferdinand von Helmholtz, whose work in thermodynamics founded the "Berlin School" and influenced a generation of physicists, including Albert Einstein. Helmholtz drew the big picture, connecting entropy to the end of life:

"If the universe be delivered over to the undisturbed action of its physical processes, all force will finally pass into the form of heat, and all heat come into a state of equilibrium . . . The life of men, animals, and plants, could not of course continue if the sun had lost its high temperature . . . In short, the universe from that time forward would be condemned to a state of eternal rest."[16]

The entropy law establishes an *economy of matter in particular forms* running through organisms and environments. As the economist Herman Daly explains it, "Were it not for the entropy law, nothing would ever wear out; we could burn the same gallon of gasoline over and over, and our economic system could be closed with respect to the rest of the natural world." Carey denied the one law that enforced a matter/energy budget in favor of one that made scarcity look like an illusion. But sense his predicament. Thermodynamics asked him to make an enormous shift in thinking. In the words of the economist Nicholas Georgescu-Roegen, "It was quite difficult not only for physicists but also for other men of science to reconcile themselves to the blow inflicted on the supremacy of mechanics by the science of heat."[17] Carey and others of his ilk settled comfortably into their colossal intellectual error, holding fast to a mechanistic model that, as Georgescu-Roegen put it, "can neither account for the existence of enduring qualitative changes in nature nor accept this existence as an independent fact." An economy so understood is "an isolated, self-contained and ahistorical process . . . a circular flow between production and consumption with no outlets and no inlets."[18]

Georgescu-Roegen was talking not about kooky nineteenth-century political economy of the kind Carey practiced, but about economics as we know it. In 1871 a British chemist named William Stanley Jevons made the startling as-

sertion that difficult-to-define terms such as utility and value
"admit of mathematical analysis and expression." He converted the old categories into quantities that could be manipulated with calculus, the branch of mathematics that deals
with the way sets of variables are affected by small changes.
Though Jevons had no reason to believe that utility behaved
just as energy did, that very equation became the basis of
neoclassical theory. In other words, as unlikely as it seems,
Jevons and those who followed him derived the first modern
school of economic thought from their reading of mid-
nineteenth-century physics. "To put it bluntly," writes Philip
Mirowski, "the progenitors of neoclassicism copied down the
physical equations and just changed the names attached to
the variables." The practice of economics became the manip-
ulation of these hazy variables, a method that isolated it still
further from the exploding capacity of the economy to
change the environment. By accepting physics as a metaphor
and a set of mathematical practices, economists developed a
system of analysis that, while it seemed to explain capitalist
motion, created a world unto itself, a Plato's Cave in which
shadows passed for reality.[19]

Economists must have sensed the danger posed by feedback from the environment. In their way of thinking, stretch-
ing back to the Scottish Enlightenment, civil society *could
not change into anything else*. It had nowhere to go but out,
and its outward development confirmed the superiority of
modernity. What if expansion ceased to be profitable? What if
growth in population, territory, markets, and infrastructure
maxed out because nature rudely interjected itself? Observers
had long said that civil society could not endure a falling rate
of profit, the great fear being havoc as defining institutions,
such as the division of labor, stagnated under high factor
costs. They saw the mechanism breaking down and people
scattering, going to war with each other, sliding back into

barbarism. Every financial hiccup during the nineteenth century provoked this kind of rhetoric. Anthropologist Joseph A. Tainter arrives at nearly the same conclusion. Tainter studies the collapse of complex societies and identifies one symptom common to the Romans and the Mayans: diminishing returns to complexity itself. "After a certain point," he writes, "increased investments in complexity fail to yield proportionately increasing returns. Marginal returns decline and marginal costs rise. Complexity as a strategy becomes increasingly costly." Growth is one way that complex societies maintain returns to complexity, but to regard it as the rampart of state and good order would be to accept an antiquated model that no longer serves our needs. Thinking within the theory of stages diminishes the possibility of change that would avoid collapse.[20]

Ignoring extinction and pollution allowed economic thinkers to shield their beloved model, but it put them into deep water without chart or compass. We are all in the same water now. The only monsters really to be feared are the ones we allow to feed in the depths of ideology. According to the critic Bruno Latour, all cultures create hybrids between nature and culture. Stone tools are hybrids; so are practices like farming. Latour argues that modern people deny the existence of their hybrids while nontechnological peoples positively obsess over theirs, installing layer upon layer of ritual to circumscribe forces with the power to destroy them. Nonmoderns commonly believe "in the impossibility of changing the social order without modifying the natural order—and vice versa." For moderns, on the other hand, "the social order never turns out to correspond, point for point, with the natural order." But the hybrids are popping up everywhere, in melting tundras and bleached-out coral reefs. Jared Diamond's version of collapse emphasizes environmental catastrophe and the odd way that people adhere to the very practices that lead to crisis. In other words, he looks to human behavior, not systematic malaise, noting, "The modern world provides us with abundant secular examples of admirable values to which we cling under conditions where those values no longer make sense . . . At what point do we as individuals prefer to die than to compromise and live?"[21]

The political economists left us an overarching model of the economy that might not adapt to the end of expansion, along with an ideology of progress that cannot assimilate its own negative effects. Not the best situation. The feedback is getting stronger that economic growth, as the sign of some ultimate stage of social evolution, cannot be maintained. If that's true, how might we confront it? Collapse might seem a little too dire to seriously contemplate, but what if the social benefits of growth have already expired even though GDP keeps increasing? What if growth no longer delivers the kind of democratic returns it once did, back when every settler had his piece of Ohio? Who will continue to place confidence in a system that serves only the interests of a tiny fraction of the population? Social justice, as well as environmental survival, might demand that we embrace alternatives to the mechanistic model.

•

The thinker who first proposed a rigorous economics of limits was Georgescu-Roegen. Born in Romania, he studied at Bucharest and the Sorbonne, earned a Ph.D. at the age of twenty-four, and briefly served in the Romanian government before defecting with his wife in the cargo hold of a ship bound for Istanbul. Ending up in the United States at Vanderbilt University in the 1950s, Georgescu-Roegen defected again—this time from one of the central assumptions of economics: that growth can continue indefinitely. According to him, economies, like everything else in the universe, are governed by thermodynamics, and he dedicated his career to proving "that the economic process as a whole is not a mechanical phenomenon." Over the next thirty years, he built a case for the biological and physical foundations of economics. Beyond a certain point, he claimed, an economy can continue to grow only by consuming its natural capital, because any rate of increase beyond the regenerative capacity of ecosystems spends them down. He spoke to environmentalists throughout the 1970s, but no one else listened. No idea could have been more unpopular in policy circles during the 1980s than that of physio-economic limits.

By the time he died, in 1994, Georgescu-Roegen had taught a generation of students. One of them was Herman Daly. Daly's father owned a hardware store in Houston, and he grew up with an abiding sense of practicality. At Rice University he discovered economics while searching for intellectual unity between the sciences and the humanities. Daly styled himself after John Kenneth Galbraith, editor of *Fortune* magazine, professor at Harvard, and adviser to John F. Kennedy. But he also admired a more unconventional scholar: Kenneth E. Boulding, who, in addition to writing a multivolume work on international trade, attempted to connect biology and economics. It was Boulding who said, "Anyone who believes exponential growth can go on forever in a finite world is either a madman or an economist." In the meantime, Daly had discovered Mexico, beginning a long relationship with Latin America and eventually writing a dissertation on Brazil. Then in 1988 came an opportunity to practice development economics at the World Bank as senior economist in the Environment Department.

Everyone at the World Bank seemed to be talking about sustainable development, and Daly fitted right in, but he soon discovered that the institution's commitment went only so far. "Every time I tried to give the concept a little bit of an edge, they would back off. They would say that sustainable development was just good development," which meant they thought they had been doing it all along. Daly struggled to move the bank toward a more contained understanding of GDP, noting that the true meaning of income is the interest earned on some form of capital. He urged a lending policy that would encourage nations to manage their natural capital in the same way that universities manage their endowments—for interest at some safe rate of return. Liquidating natural capital (through a process called export) in order to pay off the World Bank is like selling land to prevent starvation. The result is dependence. But the typical understanding of GDP regards consumption as income. Central American farmers who deforest a hillside to extend their cultivation add to GDP even though the ensuing erosion will quickly cause their yields to plummet, even though the lack of firewood will send them farther from home in search of fuel. Pointing out these contradictions to those who did not want to hear him wore Daly out after six years. "The World Bank's commitment to economic growth, free trade, and globalization," he said at his retirement, "overwhelmed its concern for environment and equity."[22]

Landing at the University of Maryland, he began to sketch out an adverse theory of industrial economy. He set out to dismantle a simple premise, one that Adam Smith first proposed in *The Wealth of Nations*—that man-made capital (fishing boats) could substitute for natural capital (cod). The way most economists think of it, only energy and technology place limits on production. If you want to harvest more wood, build a better chain saw; to pump more oil, drill more wells; to get more food, invent pest-resistant plants and fertilizers. That logic thrived on new frontiers, but there are signs that returns to labor have begun to flatten out. Fish provide an example. The planetary marine catch increased from nineteen million tons per year in 1950 to eighty million tons by 1990. Seventy percent of the world's saltwater fish species are now considered overexploited or fully exploited. The harvest of Atlantic cod, in particular, peaked in 1970, after which it began to decline. In 1991 the cod fishery collapsed. Fleets went out to the Georges Bank off the coast of Newfoundland to find nothing. The government of Newfoundland has closed its two largest fisheries intermittently since the early 1990s to build the spawning biomass to its long-term average. The catch will remain at some level below the average rate of reproduction. It will never again exceed it. Fishermen now catch fewer fish than they did in 1950, when the expansion began. The limiting factor, in other words, is no longer tools but natural capital. The cod themselves now determine the size of the industry. In an economic sense, the cod fishery is in stasis.[23]

Newfoundland and its fishing communities represent a shift in the direction and purpose of investment that might soon spread to the entire economy. Since the 1770s, capitalists have learned to invest in the limiting factor of production in order to maximize its productivity. In the past, that always meant improving the tools of the take, but it now means something different—enhancing natural capital, the new limiting factor. Daly finds a precedent in "fallowing," or the practice of letting land regenerate after a period of cultivation. Fallowing is investment in short-term nonproduction in order to maintain long-term yields. Daly applies the same idea to every renewable resource: "Leave it alone. Let it grow in order to slow or reduce the exploitation. This conforms perfectly to the economic definition of investment—a reduction in present consumption in order to increase a future capacity to consume." Of course, this is not the way that economists—let alone bankers or bond traders—think of investment. Fallowing is investment without growth, and in our current economic mind-set, lack of growth is tantamount to the end of progress.

•

There has always been an alternative. The sphere of growth can be redefined as unrealized efficiency. Eliminate waste in production. Make cars lighter to save fuel. Replace petroleum-burning engines with hydrogen-burning fuel cells. Better yet, redesign the factory itself to acknowledge that all production is a subsystem of the larger biophysical system of the earth. Make its materials recyclable and its by-products ecologically absorbable so that manufacturing becomes environmentally benign. It's called industrial ecology, and it has been waiting for its moment for half a century. That moment has arrived.

In the 1990s a group of companies in Kalundborg, Denmark, began to organize their waste collectively, regarding every discarded drop and vapor as having a possible use. Steam from the power station generates electricity at the refinery; sulfur from the refinery arrives at the plant that makes sulfuric acid; sludge from Novo Nordisk is trucked to farmers for fertilizer. The technical coordination between engineers at the eight or more factories that make up the Kalundborg Centre for Industrial Symbiosis is unprecedented. Many of the transfers take place through miles of conduits that connect every company to every other. Industrial ecology, as practiced at Kalundborg, aims to reengineer production—and eventually the larger economy—into a perfect reflection of the biosphere.

Waste might seem integral to any system of production,

but it's actually a recent invention. Until the eighteenth century, all by-products (things like animal dung, corn husks, and iron slag) either had their own use or returned to the landscape without causing trouble. But molecules like Styrofoam, CFCs, carbon dioxide, and most plastics cannot be broken down into their basic elements for decades, if at all, and they do cause trouble. This is waste—the externalizing of industrial by-products that don't reduce to basic matter. In the future envisioned by industrial ecologists, there would be no waste. Factories would metabolize like forests—endlessly cycling energy and nutrients. Kalundborg became a kind of Disney World for efficiency-seeking industrial engineers on every continent. Industrial ecology promises big. Its radical resource efficiency offers an end to scarcity. In this optimistic scenario, if companies and consumers form networks of material recycling, then nothing should ever be depleted and the foundations of growth would be secure.

Thomas Graedel, an industrial ecologist at Yale University, is tracking down the present address of the world's metals—all the copper, zinc, silver, nickel, and lead dug out of the ground over the last century and made into electric motors and logic boards. He wants to know how much copper you have in your garage and how much is stored in landfills all over the world. In other words, he's interested in big material cycles. Graedel is a tidy man, with thinning hair and a kindly manner. The framed poster of a blue Ferrari in his office does nothing to suggest a wild side. It is easy to see his sense of personal economy in his definition of industrial ecology: "to enable technology to provide the goods and services that people want and need without depleting resources and without generating impacts on the planet more severe than the planet can accommodate." That leaves space for growth to continue, says Graedel, and if it is truly rendered benign, it should have "no planetary impact"—but the way is not clear.

The problem has to do with costs. "We're never going to run out of aluminum; we're never going to run out of iron. We're never going to run out of them, because it might become too expensive to use them." Graedel cautions that—particularly with aluminum—the energy required to extract and manufacture it could make it prohibitive. As for substitutes, sometimes all the options are lousy. "The glib idea that when we need it, technology will save us assumes that we can find a substitute when we need it." A laptop computer contains sixty elements—two-thirds of the periodic table. Each element plays a specific role, yet some, like copper and platinum, are getting harder to find.

In other words, we don't need to run out of something in order for it to cause a crisis. That might not seem alarming when the subject is nickel, but what about petroleum? Finding a substitute for oil is already shaping into a race to preserve civilization. For two centuries, almost all our energy has come from highly combustible fossilized hydrocarbons. They pack a tremendous punch for their weight and volume, and they do this (historically at least) at a remarkably low cost. Fossil fuels underwrite our material lives. We hardly notice when trucks travel thousands of miles hauling containers filled with plastic lawn furniture made in China, and we don't think twice about shopping for South African oranges in air-conditioned supermarkets before driving half an hour to get home. Yet if petroleum keeps rising over $100 per barrel, our perfectly ordinary, highly dispersed, energy-intensive economic geography will become unworkable. Oil is not simply implicated in everything we call growth—there has never been growth without it.

The world consumption of oil is eighty-four million barrels a day. American cars alone consume nine million. Yet even though the end of its production is in sight, there is no substitute for oil—*nothing* stands ready to replace even

10 percent of present consumption. Hydrogen needs to be rendered by using solar power; otherwise it's just a highly refined form of petroleum. Producing biofuels equal to the present demand for crude oil would require millions of acres of forested and cultivated land, competing for space with biodiversity and food production. Dedicating a scarce resource (land) to an open-ended demand (energy) would be crazy. Sunlight is the most promising resource, for its relatively high density, but our civilization depends on much higher densities. It is now possible to convert solar radiation to electricity at densities of 20 to 60 W/m^2. That's roughly equal to the concentration in most homes. Intensify the use, however, and the energy concentration soars. The average office building concentrates 200 to 400 W/m^2. The average factory operates on 300 to 900 W/m^2. Imagine the amount of space necessary to convert any metropolitan area to even 25 percent solar power if every common lightbulb needs its own square meter of photovoltaic panels. Nuclear energy might make a comeback, but its safety and waste problems are still daunting.[24]

Energy is important to the future of growth for another reason. The radical efficiency necessary to draw out the lifetime of hard-to-replace resources will demand power far beyond what the sun, hydrogen, or wind can now provide. Any new process or jump in efficiency will, in all likelihood, require more energy. Daly is skeptical that enough will be available to achieve the efficiencies crucial to industrial ecology, calling the entire project into question. "Industrial ecology can do a lot of good," he says, "but the energy it will take to approach 100 percent recycling of material will be a ruinous cost. Industrial ecology won't save growth."

•

The stakes are high, especially for those social observers who believe that democracy itself depends on sustained economic growth. This is Benjamin Friedman's argument in *The Moral Consequences of Economic Growth*, perhaps the most comprehensive rendition of the idea, dating from the eighteenth century, that growth benefits the Many, not just the Few. "I believe," he writes, "that the rising intolerance and incivility and the eroding generosity and openness that have marked important aspects of American society in the recent past have been, in significant part, a consequence of the stagnation of American middle-class living standards during much of the last quarter of the twentieth century." Friedman makes a great deal of the correlation between the economy and crime, seeing an upsurge in hostility and anger among Americans whenever incomes and GDP flatten out, including anti-immigrant rhetoric, private militias, domestic terrorism, and waning sympathy for the poor. His claims, however, feel thin. A number of the ills he names (private militias, say, or anti-immigrant sentiment) appeared or worsened during Ronald Reagan's presidency, when GDP increased by a remarkable 3.8 percent a year. Or take murder: when the economy surged after the end of World War II, murder surged with it, climbing from 4.6 per 100,000 people in 1950 to 10.2 in 1980, and after showing no clear trend during the booming 1980s, it declined to levels not seen since the 1960s. The economy cannot explain both the rise and the fall.[25]

A more troubling question is whether growth improves the lives of the poor. For the 80 percent of households in the middle and bottom of the income scale, after-tax income increased only slightly, remained the same, or *fell* between 1977 and 1999. Adjusted for inflation, incomes for the poorest Americans fell substantially. But for the 20 percent of households at the top of the scale, after-tax income increased 43 percent during the same period. Among the top 1 percent, it increased 115 percent, more than doubling. During the 1990s, the trend in uneven concentration intensified. By 2004, the share of wealth controlled by the bottom 80 percent had fallen from 19 percent to 15.3 percent, with the difference shifting to the rich.[26] In the meantime, according to the Economic Policy Institute, the *average* CEO income increased to more than eight hundred times the minimum wage. The detachment of executives from any duty to the public weal has resulted in spectacular scandals that have left thousands without secure retirement funds. "If our growth falters," worries Friedman, "the deterioration of American society will, I fear, worsen," but it seems that he is only looking at the lower reaches of the income scale for criminality. At the top, growth has created the circumstances for that deterioration.[27]

If growth does not result in social equality and the reduction of poverty, it abdicates its single social justification. It would then be left naked as a process of wealth creation for the upper 1 percent of the population, which is exactly what appears to have taken place. Two economists, Emmanuel Saez and Thomas Piketty, discovered greater income disparity than anyone imagined by looking *within the top 1 percent of households*. As it turns out, the top 0.1 percent of earners made 6.8 percent of the nation's pretax income in 2004, an increase from 4.7 percent in 1994. "Economic growth in most of the world is so inequitable," cautions economist Robert U. Ayres, "that by far the largest share of the benefits is being appropriated by a tiny group of those who were already rich or well-connected . . . Growth as measured by GDP, even where it is more than keeping up with population, is not producing comparable increases in real social welfare. In short, the present pattern of growth is socially unsustainable."[28]

Depending on how we measure it, the economy might

not be growing anyway. The dollar value of GDP has increased at an average rate of 2.5 percent since 1973, but for millions of Americans the *net* growth—made up of things like higher real wages, improved infrastructure, widespread financial security, and a higher quality of life—is stuck. The measure of GDP itself, as critical economists have said for decades, makes no sense. An automobile accident, a sudden rise in cancer patients, a toxic-waste spill—all of them require services to be rendered, wages to be paid, and materials to be acquired, so they all contribute to GDP, while the steady erosion of a country's resources, its species, and its open spaces, all crucial assets, do not detract from it. In 1932 the economist Arthur Cecil Pigou described the way GDP depends on entities it does not value: "It is a paradox . . . that the frequent desecration of national beauty through the hunt for coal or gold, or through more blatant forms of commercial advertisement, must, on our definition, leave the national dividend intact." Growth at such an expense is not *economic*, as Daly puts it, but *uneconomic*—greater in its negative externalities than its positive returns. As Bill McKibben writes, "Growth is no longer making people wealthier, but instead generating inequality and insecurity."[29]

That view may not be popular, but it is gaining. Robert Solow, who won the Nobel Prize in economics in 1987 for innovations in growth theory, now calls himself "agnostic" as to whether or not growth can continue, and he is cheerfully willing to contemplate a zero-growth economy. As Solow said to me, "There is no reason at all why capitalism could not survive without slow or even no growth. I think it's perfectly possible that economic growth cannot go on at its current rate forever." This does not mean that productivity will cease to increase our quality of life; it means that people might find it increasingly costly to turn productivity into the kinds of things they are now accustomed to buying with their earnings. "It is possible," says Solow, "that the United States and Europe will find that as the decades go by, either continued growth will be too destructive to the environment and they are too dependent on scarce natural resources or they would rather use increasing productivity in the form of leisure . . . There is nothing intrinsic in the system that says it cannot exist happily in a stationary state."[30]

A *stationary state*. The term comes from John Stuart Mill, who argued in 1848 that "the increase of wealth is not boundless." Economists should know, said Mill, that "at the end of what they term the progressive state lies the stationary state, that all progress in wealth is but a postponement of this." A steady-state economy no longer increases its physical stock of wealth. We could take only 1 or 2 percent of a forest or fishery a year without taking a bite out of its reproductive capacity, a rate that would "bring finance into balance with the real underpinnings of finance," according to Daly. He comes up with the same numbers to describe the impact of future productivity as a result of technological innovation. It is also on the order of 1 or 2 percent a year, though it could go higher. The big lesson is that technological civilizations have arcs of expansion, and though for the last 250 years they have created an enormously more complex material world than that of hunter-gatherers, in the end both reach their stationary states—the point at which they cannot expand without grinding down natural capital.[31]

We will likely look back at the period between 1600 and 2050 as the Era of Expansion. The first date marks the beginning of surplus agriculture in England, when its population began to climb out of famine, when agrarian people all over the world began a period of wildfire frontier settlement, and when capitalism appeared. The second date marks the year when present trends in consumption will reach a level equal to double the earth's capacity, requiring a second planet. The UN projects that humans will increase by 36 percent between now and 2050, to around nine billion. Rising population will offset any savings from improved efficiency and any reduction in per capita consumption. According to World Watch, even if Americans were to eat 20 percent less beef by 2050, total U.S. beef consumption would be five million tons *greater* in 2050 simply because there will be more people. Economists have long insisted that wealth is not a zero sum, that it can be created. Yet if the biophysical capacity of the earth comes under strain, the wealth of one nation could come at the expense of others. China and India now demand an increasing share of the energy and resources that the United States and Europe once claimed for themselves, triggering unprecedented oil prices that reverberate throughout the economy.

Faith in economic growth ignited during a certain moment, when a providential belief in the limitlessness of the earth coalesced around the accelerated production made possible by fossil fuels. Progress toward salvation became the progress of a more durable existence. Growth has since become a conditiion of the political order, but that way of thinking might not survive much longer. In a no-growth society, adaptability will be more important than wealth. People of the developed economies will eventually need to attend to long-standing scarcities in the countries that have financed their expansion. Entrepreneurs will think up innovative services and invest in industrial-scale recycling, because expansion in any industry will require the bidding away of materials from others. Commodity exchanges will be flush with metals mined from landfills. Companies will lease rather than sell their products in order to keep hold of highly valued inputs. None of this is as far-fetched as the notion that we can project the status quo into the distant future.

Friedman fastens our freedom and equality to our abundance, but the circumstances that made possible the twentieth-century formula are quickly vanishing. If ecological economists are right, we simply have no choice but to think about how to maintain social tolerance without continued physical expansion. There's no guarantee that an economic transition won't bring resentment and hatred to the surface. Resisting them will be the greatest challenge, as it was during the Great Depression, when totalitarianism from the right and left attracted vocal advocates. But we can take solace in the simple truth that *societies change* and that no one can be aware of all the events and movements that cause change. We can, however, recognize the signs and act on them. The danger in any transition is a vacuum in political leadership that causes people to feel alone, afraid, and responsible for forces beyond their control.

At Costco, when I ask a manager to point out items that are made from recycled material or that save energy—items, in other words, that represent fewer inputs from the environment and higher efficiency—he looks deep into the cavern before answering, as though he is divining something in the shelves. "We have over three thousand items here," he says finally. He directs me to look at individual packages. I notice a number of Energy Star appliances, a selection of compact fluorescent lightbulbs, and salmon farmed in Canada. But not one of the paper products indicates post-consumer content, and just about everything else is made from (or powered by) petroleum. The twenty or so items that represent "less" and not "more" offset about as much as a kitchen sponge tossed into the Atlantic. And yet Costco is not an offender so much as a bellwether, indicating that Americans are heading in two directions at once. They have accepted efficiency as the soul of what it means to be green, but they have not yet recognized a biophysical limit on the quantity of their consumption. The end of growth will not mean the end of progress, to the extent that we can redefine progress as consisting of something other than accumulation. Instead, we can accept our limitations, view progress as the creation of efficiency rather than wealth, and work for just institutions even when lean times come.

Notes

Prologue: Double the Economy!
1. Transcript of the debate between Al Gore and Jack Kemp (October 9, 1996), Commission on Presidential Debates, www.debates.org/pages /trans96c.html. Author Brian Czech was also watching, and Kemp made the same impression on him. Czech refers to the debate at the beginning of *Shoveling Fuel for a Runaway Train.*
2. There were insightful people and those who responded to crisis (like John Evelyn, who wrote on the air pollution in the city of London in 1661 and whose book, *Sylva, or a Discourse on Forest Trees*, urged reforestation on private land to provide wood for the Royal Navy). Still, economic thinkers tended to maintain their position, as though they had some stake in an open-ended system.

1: A Philosophical Machine
1. Etzler, *New World, or, Mechanical System*, in *Collected Works of John Adolphus Etzler*, with an introduction by Joel Nydahl, 4. Unless otherwise indicated, all references to Etzler's books come from this collection of facsimile reproductions.
2. Coxe, *Statement of the Arts*, liv–lxi; Allen, *Science of Mechanics*, iv; Gellner, *Plough, Sword, and Book*, 140. Paul Gilmore argues that "the idea that new technologies might create true equality and true union may seem utopian, or idealist. But in the 1830s and 1840s these technologies were imagined as potentially transforming the social world by changing the way we view and inhabit it. That they did not become the liberating gods Emerson imagines poets to be means not that his

and others' hopes were unfounded but that a true opportunity was missed." Gilmore, "Mechanical Means."

3. Daly, *Steady-State Economics*, 20–28; A. Smith, *Wealth of Nations*, Book II, Chapter 3, Paragraph 6 (this form of identification refers to the Internet edition of this source and all others so identified); Marx, *Capital* (Penguin), "The Process of the Accumulation of Capital," 742. The historian Ellen Meiksins Wood writes, "Capitalism can and must constantly expand in ways and degrees unlike any other social form. It can and must constantly accumulate, constantly search out new markets, constantly impose its imperatives on new territories and new spheres of life, on all human beings and the natural environment." E. M. Wood, *Origin of Capitalism*, 97, and "The Communist Manifesto After 150 Years," *Monthly Review* 50 (May 1998), viewable at www.monthlyreview.org/598wood.htm.

4. The more recent definition of civil society emphasizes tolerance, the rule of law over personality or religion, and democratic process. I don't mean to undermine that definition one bit. The association of civil society with capitalism and markets is just as old. As for the theory of stages, even the people who told it knew it for what it was. Jean-Jacques Rousseau began his "Discourse on the Origin of Inequality" by first "setting aside all the facts, because they do not affect the question." Don't call this history, said Rousseau, but a series of "*hypothetical* and conditional reasonings, better fitted to clarify the nature of things than to expose their actual origin."

5. Gellner, *Plough, Sword, and Book*, 140–43. For a discussion of stages see Tainter, *Collapse of Complex Societies*.

6. Dunbar, *Essays on the History of Mankind*, 151; E. Everett, "The Importance of Scientific Knowledge to Practical Men and the Encouragements to Its Pursuit," *Orations and Speeches*, 275.

7. Petyt, *Britannia Languens*; Andrea Finkelstein says that Petyt was "the individual who did the most to dispel the century's fascination with bullion by replacing it with the proposition that a nation's productive capacity (its resources, labor supply, and level of technology) was the only true measure of its wealth." Finkelstein, "Nicholas Barbon," 83–102; Brewer, "Adam Ferguson, Adam Smith," and see Ferguson, *Essay on the History of Civil Society*, 215; Brisbane, *Social Destiny of Man*; A. Smith, *Wealth of Nations*, Book I, Chapter 9, paragraph 6.

8. Etzler, *Two Visions*; Introduction.

9. Bach most likely wrote the organ pieces numbered BWV 532, 720, 734, 535, 572, 718, 563, and 582 in Mühlhausen, at the organ in the Divi Blasii.

10. Biographical information gathered for the author by Roswita Henning

of Stadt Mühlhausen in Thüringen in June 2006. Etzler's parents were married on August 28, 1790, and he was born in early February—five months later.

11. Blackbourn, *Conquest of Nature*, 78–85, 96–99; Etzler, *New World, or, Mechanical System*.

12. Fürstenwärther, *Der Deutsche in Nord-Amerika*.

13. Menzel, *History of Germany*, 448–50.

14. Rotteck, *General History of the World*, 270.

15. *Morning Star* (March 1, 1845).

16. Hegel, *Philosophy of Right*, Preface, footnote.

17. Hegel, *Philosophy of History*, 31, 68.

18. Hodge, "School of Hegel," 73. Following is a list of Hegel's works that Etzler and Roebling might have read: *The Science of Logic* (1812–16), *The Encyclopaedia of the Philosophical Sciences in Outline* (1817), *The Encyclopaedia of Logic* (also known as the "Shorter Logic," 1817), *The Encyclopaedia of the Philosophy of Nature* (1817), *The Encyclopaedia of the Philosophy of Spirit* (1817), *The Lectures on Natural Right and Political Science* (1817–18), and especially *The Philosophy of Right* (1821).

19. Megill, *Karl Marx*, 63.

20. Hegel, *Philosophy of Nature*, quoted in *Hegel, the Essential Writings*, 198–201.

21. Hegel, *Philosophy of History*, 69–71.

22. Feuerbach, *Essence of Christianity*, "The Being of Man in General"; Marx, letter to Arnold Ruge in the *Deutsch-Französische Jahrbücher* (September 1844), quoted in *Marx-Engels Reader*, 9.

23. Marx, *German Ideology*, 107–08. On people just getting by, see Ehrenreich, *Nickel and Dimed*. Benjamin Friedman neglects Marx's contribution to materialism in *Moral Consequences of Economic Growth*.

24. Marx, *Theses on Feuerbach*.

25. Hegel, *Philosophy of History*, 104.

26. Menzel, *History of Germany*, 448–50.

27. Steinman, *Builders of the Bridge*, 10–18.

28. For a history of that year, see Masur, *1831, Year of Eclipse*.

29. Rotteck, *General History of the World*, 340, 368; Sheehan, *German History*, 604–05.

30. Bruncken, *German Political Refugees in the United States*, 27, quoted in Brostowin, "John Adolphus Etzler," 2.

31. J. A. Roebling, *Diary of My Journey*, 25, 48. A hogshead is about 63 gallons.

32. J. A. Roebling, letter to Mr. F. Bähr. Pittsburgh, November 2, 1831 (published as "Pragmatists and Prophets"), 5–9.

33. J. A. Roebling, "The Harmonies of Creation," in the Roebling Collection, Rutgers University Library, quoted in Trachtenberg, *Brooklyn Bridge*, 40, 48. Quotation from Washington Roebling, ibid.

34. Steinman, *Builders of the Bridge*, 46, 60–65; W. Roebling, *Early History of Saxonburg*, 12.

35. Letter, September 3, 1832 (might be dated 1834), translated by Mrs. Ernest Treidel. "Harmony Society letter file." Letter from Etzler to Harmony, August 26, 1834. Old Economy Village, Ambridge, Pa.

36. *Niles Register* (May 4, 1833).

37. Pearson, *Notes during a Journey in 1821*; Brostowin, "John Adolphus Etzler," 32.

2: Paradise Materialized

1. Brostowin, "John Adolphus Etzler," 34.

2. Condorcet, *Historical View of the Progress of the Human Mind*, 4–5.

3. Brisbane, *Social Destiny of Man*, 2. Lewis Mumford called Fourier's *Nouveau Monde* "a book whose wide influence has hardly yet been adequately estimated or understood." Mumford, *City in History*, 594.

4. *The Phalanx* 1 (New York, October 6, 1843), 16; *London Phalanx* 64 (December 1842), 221.

5. Quoted in *The Phalanx* 1 (May 28, 1845), 348. Much of this came from a narrow reading of Fourier that stressed the practical aspects of his radical philosophy. Brisbane edited Fourier by cutting out the free love, the denial of sin, and the condemnation of capitalism (socially offensive even to Boston transcendentalists) to produce a kind of road map to utopia. American "Associationists" did not denounce the competitive aspects of industrial capitalism, as Fourier did, but rather the "killing cares, harassing anxieties, hopes blasted, and unforeseen reverses and ruin," as Horace Greeley put it. Europeans might have been exploited, but Americans suffered the "callous selfishness" and "petty cunning" of business. Americans also grappled with the religious implications of Fourierism, asking whether or not it would blend with Protestantism. Horace Greeley, "Land Reform," *Hints Toward Reforms* (New York, 1850), quoted in Guarneri, "Importing Fourierism to America," 581–94.

6. With the exception of John Stuart Mill, Karl Marx, or any of the followers of Malthus.

7. All quotations preceding the sections of this chapter are from Etzler's *Paradise*, Part 1, unless otherwise indicated. See 3, 43–45 and Part 2, 6.

8. Etzler, *Two Visions*, 7.

9. Etzler, *Paradise*, 4.

10. Feynman, Leighton, and Sands, *Feynman Lectures on Physics*, quoted in Pielou, *Energy of Nature*, 5.

11. Pielou, *Energy of Nature*, 22; Smil, *Energy at the Crossroads*, 240–41.

12. Carnot, *Reflections on the Motive Power of Heat*. Carnot suggested, without exactly stating, the two laws of thermodynamics.

13. Ewbank, *Position of Our Species in the Path of Its Destiny*, 29; *World a Workshop*, 72–73; *Inorganic Forces Ordained to Supersede Human Slavery*, 22. Ewbank served as commissioner of patents from 1849 to 1852.

14. Ewbank, *World a Workshop*, 73, 116.

15. C. Smith, *Science of Energy*, 100–11. Émile Clapeyron formulated the second law in 1834.

16. Liebig, *Organic Chemistry*. For a sample of the response to Liebig, see Rossiter, *Emergence of Agricultural Science* and the *American Journal of Agriculture and Science* 3 (January 1846).

17. Allen, *Philosophy of the Mechanics of Nature*. Allen wrote the book during the 1840s. See also his *Science of Mechanics* (1829).

18. Draper, *Treatise on the Forces Which Produce the Organization of Plants*, 1–8, 21; *Morning Star* (July 18, 1846). Etzler also said, "It is known that fertility of soil is only constituted by heat and moisture." Etzler, *New World, or, Mechanical System*, 53.

19. Putnam, *Tracts on Sundry Topics of Political Economy*, 1; Young, *Discourse*, 20; Cardozo, *Notes on Political Economy*, 1; Potter, *Political Economy*, 14.

20. Marx, *Capital* (Penguin), "The Labour Process," 284. He also noted, "Labour-power itself is, above all else, the material of nature transposed into a human organism," 323, note 29.

21. Babbage, *On the Economy of Machinery*, 120–25.

22. A. Smith, *Wealth of Nations*, Introduction, paragraph 3. As Fred Cottrell wrote in his deterministic *Energy and Society*, p. 2, "The energy available to man limits what he *can* do and influences what he *will* do." Cottrell's view is discredited by the work of Vaclav Smil.

23. "The Sources of National Wealth," *Southern Quarterly Review* 3 (April 1843), 352–67; Burges, *Address Delivered before the American Institute of the City of New York*, 51. The *North American Review* (1832) also noted, "The earth is the great primary source of the supply of human wants. It is the great laboratory, where the dust we tread upon is converted into life-sustaining nutriment. Whatever we eat, or drink, or wear, comes originally from her bosom." Potter, *Political Economy*, 14. Walker also said of political economy, hilariously, "Nothing in its fundamental principles is hypothetical or problematic."

Walker, *Science of Wealth*, 2–5. "Religion in the North American Phalanx," *New York Tribune* (1853), newspaper clipping, A. J. Mac-Donald Collection, box 1, 19–57.

24. Barbon, *Discourse of Trade*, 1–6. Barbon wanted to shoot down the conception of a nation as a household because he thought it out of step with the times. Since Aristotle, nations had been thought of as households in an economic sense, but households don't trade or produce as nations do, so Barbon was looking for a new metaphor.

25. Malthus, *Essay on the Principle of Population*, Chapter 1, paragraph 22.

26. Other influences on Malthus included David Hume, "Of the Populousness of Ancient Nations" (1752); Robert Wallace, *A Dissertation on the Numbers of Mankind in Ancient and Modern Times* (1753); A. Smith, *Wealth of Nations* (1776); Condorcet, *Progress of the Human Mind* (1795); and William Godwin, "Of Avarice and Profusion" (1797).

27. Engels, "Outlines of a Critique of Political Economy." For a brilliant argument against Malthus, see Foster, *Marx's Ecology.*

28. Cooper, *Lectures on the Elements of Political Economy*, 275.

29. E. P. Smith, *Manual of Political Economy*, 37.

30. "Religion in the North American Phalanx," *New York Tribune* (1853), newspaper clipping, A. J. MacDonald Collection, box 1, 19–57.

31. Before the Israelites could claim *eretz Israel*, the land of Israel, God told them to wipe out every state and individual existing there. "Scorched earth" refers to any method of acquiring territory by eliminating the presence of outsiders, often by destroying the land as they have known it. Seventeenth-century Spanish soldiers employed it against the Aztecs in the Valley of Mexico. Their weapon of destruction: sheep.

32. Brisbane, *Social Destiny of Man*, 240–43.

33. Etzler, *Paradise*, 62.

34. Cass, *Mexican War.* The war years stimulated Malthusian discussion throughout the country. See G. Tucker, "Malthusian Theory," 297–310. J.D.B. DeBow, *DeBow's Review* 3 (1847), 176. Polk, "Address to Congress," *Journal of the Senate* (June 1, 1841). "Growth of States," *Democratic Review* 22 (May 1848), 396–98.

35. Hietala, *Manifest Design*, passim; Harvey, *Condition of Postmodernity*, 230–35, 254–57.

36. Lause, *Young America*, 3, 35; Masquerier, *Scientific Division*, 10.

37. Etzler, *Paradise*, 43.

38. Ewbank, "Motors," 500–501. See also A. H. Everett, *Discourse*, 38–39.

39. Ensor, *Inquiry Concerning the Population of Nations*, 495–97.

40. S. Gray, *Gray versus Malthus*, 4.
41. Fogel, *Escape from Hunger*, 8–13. Some nutrition scientists now corre-
    late reduced caloric intake with longer life, and a small number of peo-
    ple in the United States starve themselves for the sake of longevity.
    How does that square with Fogel's thesis? The people who practice
    severe calorie restriction balance their intake of essential nutrients to
    the milligram, ensuring that they get the absolute minimum of what
    their bodies require for basic health. Starving people in the past had
    lopsided diets—all wheat or corn and few, if any, fresh vegetables.
    They did not starve scientifically. See also Blackbourn, *Conquest of
    Nature*, 21.
42. The point should not be stressed too hard. European cities probably
    would not have decreased in population without migration, but their
    growth remained low and mortality high until the middle of the nine-
    teenth century. See Sharlin, "Natural Decrease in Early Modern Cities:
    A Reconsideration," 126–38.
43. Allen, *Practical Tourist*, 123; Engels, *Condition of the Working Class in
    England*, 70–75.
44. *The Phalanx* (1844).
45. Luther, *Address Delivered*, 7–8.
46. Simpson, *Working Man's Manual*, 14; Man, *Picture of a Factory Vil-
    lage*.
47. Brisbane, *Concise Exposition of the Doctrine of Association*; Brisbane,
    quoted in Bronstein, *Land Reform*, 104.
48. Transon, *False Association and Its Remedy*, 51; Etzler, *New World, or,
    Mechanical System*, 49; Brisbane, quoted in *The Future* 1 (January 30,
    1841), the first number of a Fourierist paper published by Horace
    Greeley's company in New York City. "We must prove to them in var-
    ious ways," said Brisbane of capitalists, "that in civilization they are de-
    prived of all the advantages which they desire, and that in Combined
    order alone, they will possess them." Brisbane, *Social Destiny of Man*,
    357. Marx and Engels are more complicated in this regard; while they
    definitely believed in future growth, they also set out to destroy the
    old model of civil society in order to achieve a socialized wealth. Marx
    criticized utopians who, he said, did little more than try to humanize
    an institution—capital—that could not be humanized. See Marx's let-
    ter to the Icarians quoted in Harvey, *Spaces of Hope*, and Megill, *Karl
    Marx*.
49. Bastiat, *Economic Harmonies*, Chapter 3.
50. Atkinson, *Principles of Political Economy*, 36. The Malthus paraphrase
    comes from the sixth edition of the *Essay on the Principle of Population*,
    Chapter 1, paragraph 5 (Library of Economics and Liberty). See also

J. Gray, *Black Mass*, 84–87, and Polanyi, *Great Transformation*, 3. The war in Iraq is a vivid example of liberal utopianism, since its planners believed that with the declaration of a free market, Iraqis would become so enamored with consumption that they would drop all ethnic and religious differences. The rapid-fire liberalization of Russia during the 1990s is another example.

51. Emerson, "Young American."
52. Israel, *Dutch Primacy in World Trade*, 5–6.
53. A. Smith, *Wealth of Nations*, 474, 481.
54. List, *Outlines of American Political Economy*, 187; List, *National System of Political Economy*, 62; David Levi-Faur, "Friedrich List," 154–78.
55. Dixon, *American Labor*, 19–22.
56. Warden, *Statistical, Political, and Historical Account*.
57. Johnston and Williamson, "Annual Real and Nominal GDP for the United States." Woodbury, *Twenty-Second Anniversary Address*. This address is a fantastic example of how the theory of stages could be used to discuss tangible changes in the American economy, especially the interconnection between agriculture, manufacturing, and commerce.
58. G. Tucker, *Progress of the United States*, 207–08.
59. Davis, "Eleventh Anniversary Address," 1–29. On consumption, see Gilje, "Rise of Capitalism in the Early Republic" and his extensive notes. In particular, see Bushman, *Refinement of America*, and C. Clark, *Roots of Rural Capitalism*; *Scientific American* 2 (February 6, 1847); G. Tucker, *Progress of the United States*; Seaman, *Essays on the Progress of Nations*, passim.
60. Seaman, *Essays on the Progress of Nations*, 23–24, 55.
61. Davis, "Eleventh Anniversary Address," 21–29.
62. Holmes, "Population and Capital," 229; Cooper, *Lectures on the Elements of Political Economy*, 137, 272–75. Cooper said that no purely agricultural society could attain great polish and learning. His examples of manufacturing and its evils came from his brutal childhood in Manchester. Pickens, *Address on the Great Points of Difference*. For another example of the same criticism of modernity, see Kendrick, *Ancient and Modern Civilizations Contrasted*. Physiocracy refers to the economic school of the eighteenth-century French Physiocrats. They believed that all taxable value—all net produce over costs—came from agriculture and no other source. See also Hietala, *Manifest Design*.
63. Brostowin, "John Adolphus Etzler," 37.
64. D. Wood, *Trinidad in Transition*, 85. Wood cites a rare Trinidad newspaper, *Creole Bitters* (May 3, 1904), A. J. MacDonald Collection; Etzler, *Description of the Naval Automaton*, 7.

3: Utopia *Means "No Place"*

1. De Verteuil, *Germans in Trinidad*, 94. Stollmeyer published Christian G. Salzmann's *Heaven on Earth, or the Road to Happiness* (1839), Rotteck's *General History of the World*, and Brisbane's *Social Destiny of Man*.

2. I owe some of these insights to Ken Jowitt, professor of political science emeritus at the University of California, Berkeley, whose lectures I attended as an undergraduate. In another sense, Stollmeyer bears a certain resemblance to Engels, also a businessman idealist, who worked jointly with Marx but always in his shadow.

3. Etzler, *New World, or, Mechanical System*, 5, 6, 8, 66–67.

4. *Index of Patents Issued from the United States Patent Office from 1790 to 1873.*

5. *Utopia Britannica: British Utopian Experiments, 1325–1945.* www.utopia-britannica.org.uk; also see Claeys, *Utopias of the British Enlightenment*.

6. Stollmeyer in the *Northern Star*, quoted in Claeys, "John Adolphus Etzler," 375.

7. W. A. Smith, *"Shepherd" Smith the Universalist*, 215–16. For Etzler mentioned in *The London Phalanx*, see February 1842, 730, and August 1842, 80. An article in the *Living Age* (reprinted from the *Church of England Review*) mentioned that "successful trips have been made, we believe, off Margate." It is not clear whether they misreported the same test or referred to some other. *Living Age* 1 (June 29, 1844), 405.

8. *Mechanics' Magazine, Museum, Register, Journal and Gazette* (London, 1843).

9. "Mr. Etzler is expected in England in the course of the present year, by the express invitation of those who appreciate his talent and genius," wrote Hansard. "His discoveries are not more striking in their nature, than are those of the inventors and engineers of our own country; but they are upon a much more extended scale, both in their dimensions and their application." Hansard, *Hints and Reflections*, 21.

10. "Present Struggles and Their Final Issues," *Living Age* 1 (June 29, 1844): 401–06.

11. *Morning Star* (March 28, 1846).

12. Polanyi, *Great Transformation*, 30–43; Engels, *Condition of the Working Class in England*, 29, 70, 148.

13. Etzler, *New World, or, Mechanical System*, 6; ibid., 50; *Morning Star* (February 1, 1845); *Morning Star* (February 15, 1845).

14. Spell it Eutopia and it means "a good place," another of the games More plays with words and meaning.

15. *Morning Star* (December 1844); Etzler, *Emigration to the Tropical World*, 2–3. Other scientific men also calculated the intrinsic power of the tropical sun. Zachariah Allen, the Rhode Island manufacturer, figured out the mechanical force represented by the evaporation of water. Wrote Allen, "To realize the extent of the propagation of the electro-dynamic action of the sun thus effected, requires recourse to mathematical calculations. Supposing the evaporation of water by solar action on a limited belt of the earth's surface, comprised within the tropical regions alone, to be only one-eighth of an inch daily, and that this water, in the constrained static condition of vapory clouds, becomes elevated to the average height of 5,000 feet in the sky, effective impulses are thus continuously developed, which exceed 4,700,000,000 *horse power*; an extent of motive power one hundred and thirty fold greater than that of the muscular energies of all the active human population of the earth, estimating the number at 250 millions of vigorous people." Allen, *Science of Mechanics*, 30–31.

16. Dauxion-Lavaysse and Blaquière, *Statistical, Commercial, and Political Description*, 38, 45. Another story came to Etzler in 1846. A settlement of Germans from Württemberg, organized and funded by the geographer and explorer Agustin Codazzi, broke up, "the climate being too cold, the soil poor, rocky and rugged and deficient in water." *Morning Star* (September 6, 1845). Codazzi published a geography of Venezuela in 1841 and died in 1859. An institute of geography is named for him in Colombia.

17. *Morning Star* (April 1844 and October 11, 1845). The description comes from Humboldt's *Political Essay on the Kingdom of New Spain*. See also Browne, "Alexander von Humboldt as Historian of Science in Latin America," 134–39; Etzler, *Emigration to the Tropical World*, 9.

18. Stollmeyer seems to be describing the salt deposits on the surface of many arid soils caused by the evaporation of water.

19. Hegel, *Philosophy of History*, 79–80.

20. Montesquieu, *The Spirit of the Laws*, 242–47. Montesquieu was hardly the first to express such ideas, as Clarence Glacken argues in *Traces on the Rhodian Shore*, 576–87. Another view of the relation between bodies, states, and the climate is in Dunbar, *Essays on the History of Mankind*, 338.

21. Guyot, *Earth and Man*, 20–21.

22. "The differences between the North and the South are not of yesterday, nor to-day," Guyot affirmed. "If we consult the memorials of these tribes . . . it might seem that it has been the same from a time ascending beyond all our traditions." Guyot, *Earth and Man*, 247–71, 300. See also "An Account of Prof. Ritter's Geographical Labors," by

Dr. H. Bögekamp, quoted in Ritter, *Geographical Studies*, 50, 60, 317; Foster, *Marx's Ecology*, 121–22.
23. Guyot, *Earth and Man*, 330.
24. R. P. Tucker, *Insatiable Appetite*, 200–201.
25. *Morning Star* (February 15 and May 3, 1845).
26. *Morning Star* (January 3, 1846); letter from Etzler to a Mr. Greenwood, Port of Spain, February 19, 1846, in *Morning Star* (July 11, 1846). For the account of Carr, see *Morning Star* (February 17, 1846).
27. Brostowin, "John Adolphus Etzler," 308–09; *Morning Star* (November 29, 1845).
28. *Morning Star* (November 29, 1845, and January 17, 1846).
29. It goes on. Smolnikar found another engineer to fix the Satellite but then claimed that the spirit of Joseph Smith, founder of the Church of Jesus Christ of the Latter-day Saints, attacked the machine and Smolnikar himself. See *Secret Enemies of True Republicanism*. Andrew B. Smolnikar once served as vice president of the Friends of Association in the United States, along with Charles A. Dana, Horace Greeley, Brisbane, and Parke Godwin. He apparently mentioned the test of the Satellite before the general convention of the Friends of Association. See Alexander and Williams, "Andreas Bernardus Smolnikar," 50–63; *New York Tribune* (April 13, 1844).
30. *Morning Star* (April 2 and 5, 1845).
31. *Branbury Guardian* (September 25, 1845), quoted in Brostowin, "John Adolphus Etzler," 305.
32. *Morning Star* (October 11 and 18, 1845).
33. Benjamin Friedman, *Moral Consequences of Economic Growth*, passim.
34. *Morning Star* (October 11 and 18, 1845).
35. *Morning Star* (January 17, 1846).
36. *Morning Star* (February 14, 1846).
37. *Morning Star* (February 28, 1846).
38. *Morning Star* (June 20 and August 1, 1846). The second issue has an article reprinted from the *Port of Spain Gazette* by a third party who interviewed survivors in Trinidad.
39. *Morning Star* (June 20, 1846).
40. The report from the Trinidad committee was signed by William George Knox, solicitor general, and Thomas F. Johnson, agent general of immigrants, and read at a city council board meeting on April 17. *Morning Star* (August 1, 1846).
41. Powell's letter, *Morning Star* (July 4, 1846); see also *Morning Star* (September 26, 1846), where Powell calls Etzler "ashamed to meet the men he had injured"; letter from Etzler to Mr. Bredell, George-

town, British Guiana, *Morning Star* (July 4 and 18, 1846). And see the single surviving issue from 1847.

42. *Morning Star* (August 1, 1846).
43. *The Reformer* (March 6 and 13, 1847).
44. "The Sources of National Wealth," *Southern Quarterly Review* 3 (April 1843), 352–67.
45. Hegel, *Philosophy of History*, 25; Hegel, *Encyclopedia of the Philosophical Sciences*, "The Philosophy of Nature," "Preliminary Concepts," Sections 193 and 194.
46. Trachtenberg, *Brooklyn Bridge*, 60–68.
47. J. A. Roebling, quoted in Trachtenberg, *Brooklyn Bridge*, 66. For a fascinating look into Roebling's early thinking about suspension bridges, see "Some Remarks on Suspension Bridges," *American Railroad Journal* 12 (April 1, 1841).
48. Letters from Conrad F. Stollmeyer to various correspondents, from digital copies of typescript letters in the private collection of Humphrey Stollmeyer, Port of Spain, Trinidad. Rex is mentioned in *The Morning Star* (April 5, 1845) as having helped to patent the Satellite while Stollmeyer lived in Philadelphia early in the 1840s. Etzler almost certainly did not return to Philadelphia (though he might have intended to) or Rex would have conveyed that to Stollmeyer over the following years of their correspondence. Still, a Private Daniel Etzler joined the 78th Regiment of the Pennsylvania Volunteers on February 16, 1865. If Daniel was seventeen at the time he entered service, he would have been born in 1848. Daniel was probably no relation to Etzler, but no one can rule it out. Bates, *History of Pennsylvania Volunteers*, Making of America.

4: Seven Billion Billionaires

1. De Voto, "What the Next Hour Holds," 111.
2. Fuller, *Nine Chains to the Moon*. The title offered a typically obscure visual metaphor. If everyone on Earth stood on each other's shoulders, they would form nine complete chains to the moon.
3. Fuller, *Nine Chains to the Moon*, 41. See also Hatch, *Buckminster Fuller*, and Baldwin, *BuckyWorks*.
4. Fuller, *Nine Chains to the Moon*, 15–17, 256–59.
5. Lewis Mumford, in his pre–World War II career, sounded the same way. Mumford believed in a "dynamic equilibrium" and shouted out his precepts for an enlightened, technological civilization: "Economize Production! . . . Normalize Consumption! . . . Socialize Creation! . . . For however far modern science and technics have fallen short of their

inherent possibilities, they have taught mankind at least one lesson: Nothing is impossible." Mumford, *Technics and Civilization*, chapter headings and 435.

6. Frederick Starr, "American Forests: Their Destruction and Preservation," USDA, *Annual Report* (1865), 210–34, quoted in M. Williams, *Americans and Their Forests*, 393. There was another school of American political economy, and it followed Ricardo and even Malthus. See Cooper, *Lectures on the Elements of Political Economy; DeBow's Review* (1846); Conkin, *Prophets of Prosperity*; McCoy, *Elusive Republic*.

7. United States Congress, House of Representatives, 51st Congress, 1st Session, *The Forest Reserve Act* (H.R. 7254).

8. Dunlap, *Wiley's American Iron Trade Manual*; Little, *Timber Supply Question*, 4, 24.

9. On the Great Chain of Being, see Lovejoy, *Great Chain of Being*. On mechanism, see Merchant, *Death of Nature*.

10. Walker, *Science of Wealth*, 3–5. Physics and mechanism infused nineteenth-century thought. In Mary Shelley's novel of 1818, Dr. Victor Frankenstein conceives that by capturing the motive force within all life, he could animate dead flesh, and he mulled over the problem in language any mechanic would have understood: "Whence, I often asked myself, did the principle of life proceed? . . . I revolved these circumstances in my mind, and determined thenceforth to apply myself more particularly to those branches of natural philosophy which relate to physiology."

11. See Mill, *Principles of Political Economy*.

12. Carey, *Principles of Social Science*, 65–66. Carey also said, "In the physical world motion is indispensable to the existence of force. Motion, itself, is a consequence of heat. So, too, the physical and social laws being one and the same, should it be in the societary world . . . Look where we may, we find evidence of the universality of those great laws instituted for the government of matter in all its forms—heat, motion, and force, being everywhere found in the precise ratio of the development of individuality, and of the power of association and combination." Carey, *Manual of Social Science*, 391.

13. E. P. Smith, *Manual of Political Economy*, quoted in Carey, *Unity of Law*, 127. Carey wrote that the conservation of matter extended to society, calling it "not fate, but fact; not materialism, but order, organism, law, government . . . it affirms only that matter in the human form, as in the rest of the universe, is subject to positive, permanent, and universal rules of action." *Unity of Law*, 124. Carey, *Principles of Political Economy*, Vol. 3, 251–55; Carey, *Harmony of Interests*, 123; Seaman, *Essays on the Progress of Nations*, 23–24. The contrast with

Mill is striking. In 1874 Mill published a series of *Essays on Some Un-settled Questions of Political Economy*. One thing he thought unsettled was the relationship between political economy and the physical sciences. Mill had this to say: "The three laws of motion, and the law of gravitation, are common, as far as human observation has yet extended, to all matter; and these, therefore, as being among the laws of the production of all wealth, should form part of Political Economy." Or, put another way, "the laws of the production of the objects which constitute wealth, are the subject-matter both of Political Economy and of almost all the physical sciences . . . Political Economy, therefore, presupposes all the physical sciences; it takes for granted all such of the truths of those sciences as are concerned in the production of the objects demanded by the wants of mankind; or at least it takes for granted that the physical part of the process takes place somehow." Presupposing the physical sciences is not at all the same thing as admitting an identity with their laws, an idea Mill rejected. See Essay V, paragraph 19.

14. Marsh, *Man and Nature*, 134–35, 548n. Marsh is often referred to as a "utilitarian," but his ecological sensibility constantly calls utilitarian values into question. Later conservationists would see forestry and land management as measures for prolonging consumption indefinitely, even with a rising population, but this was never Marsh's point. The only way he could have arrived at his conclusions was by the close observation of living nature—by building a theory on the interaction between life and the solid earth. The quotation on interconnectedness is a paraphrase of Babbage, *The Ninth Bridgewater Treatise*, a work of natural theology.

15. Carey, *Manual of Social Science*, 47 (the reference to Tyndall might have been added by the editor of the volume); Tyndall, *Heat Considered as a Mode of Motion*, 132.

16. Hermann Ludwig Ferdinand von Helmholtz, "The Interaction of Natural Forces" (1854?), quoted in Youmans, *Correlation and Conservation of Forces*, 70, 228–29. See also Werner Ebeling and Dieter Hoffman, "The Berlin School of Thermodynamics Founded by Helmholtz and Clausius," *European Journal of Physics* 12 (January 1991), 1–9, and Cardwell, *From Watt to Clausius*. Carey had only to refer to *Chambers's Encyclopedia*, which stated the law in 1872. An article on "energy" in *The Globe Encyclopedia* (1876) contained the following: "We are compelled to accept the dissipation principle as an important law in nature," an admission followed by news of an experiment by Clerk Maxwell of Cambridge University intended to demonstrate that energy could be contained in certain situations. The experiment failed,

"overthrowing the whole of that materialism which has of late years been advocated by quasi-scientific skeptics." See Arnott, *Elements of Physics*, 272, and H. F. Walling, "The Dissipation of Energy," *Popular Science Monthly* 4 (1874), 430.

17. Georgescu-Roegen, *Entropy Law*, 141.

18. "The threat has always existed that an external intellectual discipline will contradict or falsify some crucial tenet of the abstraction designated by 'the economy.'" Mirowski, *Against Mechanism*, 108; Georgescu-Roegen, *Entropy Law*, 223. Georgescu-Roegen also said the following about the distinction between whole and part: "The complete description of Matter includes not only the property of the atom of, say, carbon, but also of those of all organizations of which carbon is a constituent part." *Entropy Law*, 116.

19. Mirowski, *Against Mechanism*, 31 and Chapter 3. Jevons explicitly applied mechanism to human behavior in the marketplace, writing, "Life seems to be nothing but a special form of energy which is manifested in heat and electricity and mechanical force . . . Must not the same inexorable reign of law which is apparent in the motions of brute matter be extended to the human heart?" See also Nadeau, *Wealth of Nature*, 41, and Jevons, *Principles of Science*, 735–36. As Georgescu-Roegen put it, "by the time Jevons and Walras began laying the cornerstones of modern economics, a spectacular revolution in physics had already brought the downfall of the mechanistic dogma . . . the curious fact is that none of the . . . model builders seem to have been aware at any time of this downfall." The trouble with economics, according to Paul P. Christensen, is "the inconsistency between the neoclassical principle of marginal productivity of individual inputs and the biophysical principles governing real-world production activities, in particular the first and second laws of thermodynamics. It would be inappropriate to base production theory and environmental economics on concepts which are incompatible with the operations of the physical and biological world." Paul P. Christensen, "Early Links Between Sciences of Nature and Economics: Historical Perspectives for Ecological and Social Economics," in *The Economics of Nature and the Nature of Economics*, 16. Jevons is sometimes credited with introducing scarcity into economy with his book *The Coal Question*, but few have understood his project. Jevons believed markets to be inherently stable and sought any possible explanation for their failure in causes outside of markets. For a full discussion, see Mirowski, *Against Mechanism*, Chapter 1.

20. Marx makes reference to the possibility in a number of places, especially in Volume Three of *Capital*. Referring to the fear of collapse among capitalists, he writes, "The main point in their horror over the

falling rate of profit is the feeling that capitalist production meets in the development of productive forces a barrier which has nothing to do with the production of wealth as such; and this peculiar barrier testifies to the finiteness and the historical, merely transitory character of capitalist production." See Marx, *Capital*, Vol. 3, Part 2, Chapter 15; Williams, *Lectures on Political Principles*, 85. One American said this: "This division of labour is so essential to civilized man, that whenever we abandon it we must return to barbarism." *Journal of the American Institute* 4 (October 1838), 1–29. Tainter, *Collapse of Complex Societies*, 93. Tainter defines complexity as multiple social roles, hierarchies, and subunits such as villages, provinces, or states. There have been complex societies that have never had economic growth as we have known it.

21. Latour, *We Have Never Been Modern*, 41–42; Diamond, *Collapse*, 432–33.
22. Interview with Herman Daly, March 19, 2007.
23. World Bank, *Saving Fish and Fishers*.
24. Smil, *Energy at the Crossroads*, 240–41. To get some sense of the space required, consider this little irony: a massive solar park—the largest in the world at this writing—recently went into operation outside of Mühlhausen, Etzler's hometown. The Bavaria Solarpark has a maximum capacity of 10MW (10 million watts) from solar panels installed in three locations. The panels cover a total surface area of $250,000\text{m}^2$, the equivalent of about 62 acres. The efficiency comes out to around 40 watts generated per square meter—enough to power a lightbulb. But an average skyscraper concentrates 200 watts (at the low end) in 6,000 square meters (at the low end), or 1.2 million total watts. So the Bavarian Solarpark has the capacity to power up eight average-sized office buildings.
25. Crime Statistics from Bureau of Justice Crime Data Brief, "Homicide Trends in the United States: 2000 Update," www.ojp.usdoj.gov/bjs /pub/pdf/htus00.pdf.
26. Shapiro and Greenstein, *Widening Income Gulf*; Economic Policy Institute, *The State of Working America*, 251.
27. From a graph based on crime statistics available from the FBI: www.fbi .gov/ucr/05cius/data/table_01.html. The graph itself may be found under "U.S. Violent Crime," Wikipedia.org.
28. Leonhardt, "New Inequality"; Robert U. Ayres, "The Need For a New Growth Paradigm," *The Economics of Nature*, 111.
29. Pigou, *Economics of Welfare*, quoted in Colin Clark, *Conditions of Economic Progress*, 18–21; McKibben, *Deep Economy*, 1.
30. Interview, Robert Solow, April 20, 2007.

31. Marx also had a sense that little really separated the materialism of hunters and moderns. In the third volume of *Capital*, he wrote, "Just as the savage must wrestle with Nature to satisfy his wants, to maintain and reproduce life, so must civilised man, and he must do so in all social formations and under all possible modes of production." *Capital*, Vol. 3, Part 7, Chapter 48, paragraph 13.

Bibliography

Manuscript Collections

A. J. MacDonald Collection of Utopian Materials. Beinecke Rare Book and Manuscript Library, Yale University.

Conrad F. Stollmeyer Collection, in the private holdings of the Stollmeyer Family, Port of Spain, Trinidad.

Harmony Society Letter File, Old Economy Village, Ambridge, Pennsylvania.

Significant Internet Resources

Center on Budget and Policy Priorities. www.cbpp.org.

Hegel by HyperText. www.marxists.org/reference/archive/hegel.

Historical Census Browser. University of Virginia Library. fisher.lib.virginia .edu/collections/stats/histcensus.

Library of Congress. American Memory. Evolution of the Conservation Movement. memory.loc.gov.

Library of Economics and Liberty. www.econlib.org.

The Making of America. University of Michigan. moa.umdl.umich.edu.

The Making of the Modern World. The Goldsmiths'-Kress Library of Economic Literature 1450–1850. www.gale.com/ModernWorld.

Marxists.org. www.marxists.org.

Project Gutenberg. www.gutenberg.org.

Project Muse. muse.jhu.edu.

The State of Working America. www.stateofworkingamerica.org.

Periodicals
American Journal of Agriculture and Science
American Railroad Journal
Branbury Guardian (England)
Democratic Review
The Future
Journal of the American Institute
Journal of the Senate
Living Age
The London Phalanx
Mechanics' Magazine (London)
The Morning Star
New York Tribune
Niles Register
North American Review
Northern Star
The Peaceful Revolutionist
The Phalanx (New York City)
Princeton Review
The Reformer
Southern Quarterly Review

Books and Articles
Alexander, Jon, O.P., and David Williams, "Andreas Bernardus Smolnikar: American Catholic Apostate and Millennial Prophet." *American Benedictine Review* 35 (1984): 50–63.
Allen, Zachariah. *The Science of Mechanics, as Applied to the Present Improvements in the Useful Arts in Europe, and in the United States of America*. Providence, R.I., 1829.
———. *The Practical Tourist, or, Sketches of the State of the Useful Arts*. Boston, 1832.
———. *Philosophy of the Mechanics of Nature, and the Source and Modes of Action of Natural Motive-Power*. New York, 1852.
Arnott, Neil. *Elements of Physics; or, Natural Philosophy*. Philadelphia: Blanchard & Lea, 1856.
Atkinson, William. *Principles of Political Economy, or, The Laws of the Formation of National Wealth, developed by means of the Christian law of government . . . with an introduction by Horace Greeley, treating of the present state of the science of political economy*. New York, 1843. Making of the Modern World.
Babbage, Charles. *On the Economy of Machinery and Manufactures*. Philadelphia: Carey and Lea, 1832.

————. *The Ninth Bridgewater Treatise*. London, 1837.

Baldwin, J. *BuckyWorks: Buckminster Fuller's Ideas Today*. New York: Wiley, 1996.

Barbon, Nicholas. *A Discourse of Trade*. London, 1690.

Bastiat, Frédéric. *Economic Harmonies*. 1850. Trans. W. Hayden Boyers. Ed. George B. de Huszar. Reprint. Princeton, N.J.: Van Nostrand, 1964.

Bates, Samuel P. *History of Pennsylvania Volunteers, 1861–5*. Harrisburg, Pa.: State Printer, 1869–71.

Blackbourn, David. *The Conquest of Nature: Water, Landscape, and the Making of Modern Germany*. New York: W. W. Norton, 2006.

Bonnett, Alastair. *The Idea of the West: Culture, Politics and History*. London: Palgrave, 2004.

Breckman, Warren. *Marx, the Young Hegelians, and the Origins of Radical Social Theory: Dethroning the Self*. New York: Cambridge University Press, 1999.

Brewer, Anthony. "Adam Ferguson, Adam Smith, and the Concept of Economic Growth." *History of Political Economy* (Summer 1999).

Brisbane, Albert. *The Social Destiny of Man, or, Association and Reorganization of Industry*. Philadelphia: C. F. Stollmeyer, 1840.

————. *A Concise Exposition of the Doctrine of Association, or, Plan for a Reorganization of Society*. New York: J. S. Redfield, 1844.

Bronstein, Jamie L. *Land Reform and Working-Class Experience in Britain and the United States, 1800–1826*. Stanford, Calif.: Stanford University Press, 1999.

Brostowin, Patrick R. "John Adolphus Etzler: Scientific Utopian during the 1830s." Ph.D. dissertation, New York University, 1969.

Browne, C. A. "Alexander von Humboldt as Historian of Science in Latin America." *Isis* 35 (Spring 1844): 134–39.

Burges, Tristam. *Address Delivered before the American Institute of the City of New York at Their Third Annual Fair . . . Oct. 1830*. New York, 1830.

Bushman, Richard L. *The Refinement of America: Persons, Houses, Cities*. New York: Knopf, 1992.

Cardozo, Jacob Newton. *Notes on Political Economy*. 1826. Reprint. New York: A. M. Kelley, 1960.

Cardwell, D.S.L. *From Watt to Clausius: The Rise of Thermodynamics in the Early Industrial Age*. Ithaca, N.Y.: Cornell University Press, 1971.

Carey, Henry Charles. *Principles of Political Economy*. Philadelphia, 1837.

————. *The Harmony of Interests*. 2d ed. New York, 1852.

————. *Principles of Social Science*. Philadelphia, 1858.

————. *Manual of Social Science*. Philadelphia, 1872.

———. *The Unity of Law; as Exhibited in the Relations of Physical, Social, Mental and Moral Science.* Philadelphia, 1872.

Carnot, Sadi. *Reflections on the Motive Power of Heat.* 1825. Trans. R. H. Thurston. Reprint. New York: American Society of Mechanical Engineers, 1943. www.history.rochester.edu/steam.

Cass, Lewis. *The Mexican War: Speech . . . in the Senate of the United States.* Washington, 1847.

Chalmers, Thomas. *On Political Economy, in Connection with the Moral State and Moral Prospects of Society.* New York, 1832.

Claeys, Gregory. "John Adolphus Etzler, Technological Utopianism, and British Socialism: The Tropical Emigration Society's Venezuelan Mission and Its Social Context, 1833–1848." *English Historical Review* (April 1986): 351–75.

———. *Utopias of the British Enlightenment.* Cambridge: Cambridge University Press, 1994.

Clark, Christopher. *The Roots of Rural Capitalism: Western Massachusetts, 1780–1860.* Ithaca, N.Y.: Cornell University Press, 1990.

Clark, Colin. *The Conditions of Economic Progress.* London: Macmillan, 1940.

Clay, Henry. *Speech in Support of an American System for the Protection of American Industry.* Washington City, 1824.

Cleveland, Cutler J., David I. Stern, and Robert Costanza. *The Economics of Nature and the Nature of Economics.* Northampton, Mass.: Edward Elgar, 2001.

Colton, Calvin. *Public Economy for the United States.* Cincinnati, 1848.

Condorcet, Jean-Antoine-Nicolas de Caritat, Marquis de. *Outlines of an Historical View of the Progress of the Human Mind.* London, 1795. Making of the Modern World.

Conkin, Paul Keith. *Prophets of Prosperity: America's First Political Economists.* Bloomington: Indiana University Press, 1980.

Cooper, Thomas. *Lectures on the Elements of Political Economy.* Columbia, S.C., 1826.

Costanza, Robert, and Herman Daly. "Natural Capital and Sustainable Development." *Conservation Biology* 6 (March 1992): 37–46.

Cottrell, William Frederick. *Energy and Society: The Relation between Energy, Social Changes, and Economic Development.* New York: McGraw-Hill, 1955.

Coxe, Tench. *Statement of the Arts and Manufactures of the United States of America, for the Year 1810.* Philadelphia, 1814.

Cronon, William. *Nature's Metropolis: Chicago and the Great West.* New York: W. W. Norton, 1991.

Czech, Brian. *Shoveling Fuel for a Runaway Train: Errant Economists,*

Shameful Spenders, and a Plan to Stop Them All. Berkeley: University of California Press, 2000.

Daly, Herman E. *Steady-State Economics: The Economics of Biophysical Equilibrium and Moral Growth.* San Francisco: W. H. Freeman, 1977.

Dauxion-Lavaysse, J.-J., and Edward Blaquière. *A Statistical, Commercial, and Political Description of Venezuela, Trinidad, Margarita, and Tobago: Containing Various Anecdotes and Observations.* London, 1820.

Davis, John. "Eleventh Anniversary Address. Delivered before the Officers, Members, and Friends of the American Institute." *Journal of the American Institute* 4 (October 1838).

De Verteuil, Anthony. *The Germans in Trinidad.* Port of Spain: Self-published, 1994.

De Voto, Bernard. "What the Next Hour Holds." *Harper's* (June 1936): 109–11.

Diamond, Jared. *Collapse: How Societies Choose to Fail or Succeed.* New York: Penguin Books, 2005.

Dixon, James. *American Labor: Its Necessities and Prospects.* New York, 1852.

Draper, John William. *A Treatise on the Forces Which Produce the Organization of Plants.* New York, 1844.

Dunbar, James. *Essays on the History of Mankind in Rude and Cultivated Ages.* London, 1780.

Duncan, Colin A.M. "Adam Smith's Green Vision and the Future of Global Socialism." *Socialism: Future beyond Globalization.* Ed. Robert Albritton Shannon Bell, John R. Bell, and Richard Westra. Routledge: London 2004: 99–104.

Dunlap, Thomas. *Wiley's American Iron Trade Manual of the Leading Iron Industries of the United States.* New York, 1874. Making of America.

Ehrenreich, Barbara. *Nickel and Dimed: On (Not) Getting By in America.* New York: Metropolitan Books, 2001.

Eltis, Walter. *The Classical Theory of Economic Growth.* New York: St. Martin's Press, 1984.

Emerson, Ralph Waldo. "The Young American." 1844. *Ralph Waldo Emerson: Essays and Lectures.* New York: Library of America, 1983.

Engels, Friedrich. *The Condition of the Working Class in England.* 1845. Reprint. New York: Penguin Books, 1987.

———. "Outlines of a Critique of Political Economy." *Deutsch Französische Jahrbücher,* 1844. www.marxists.org/archive/marx/works/1844/df-jahrbucher/outlines.htm.

Ensor, George. *Inquiry concerning the Population of Nations: Containing a Refutation of Mr. Malthus's Essay on Population*. London, 1818.

Etzler, John Adolphus. *The Paradise Within the Reach of All Men, without Labour, by Powers of Nature and Machinery*. Pittsburgh, 1833.

————. *The New World, or, Mechanical System: To Perform the Labours of Man and Beast by Inanimate Powers, That Cost Nothing, for Producing and Preparing the Substances of Life*. Philadelphia: C. F. Stollmeyer, 1841.

————. *Emigration to the Tropical World: For the Melioration of All Classes of People of All Nations*. Surrey, England, 1844.

————. *Two Visions of J. A. Etzler: A Revelation of Futurity*. Surrey, 1844.

————. *Description of the Naval Automaton. Invented by J. A. Etzler, and Lately Patented in England, France, Holland, Belgium, and the United States of North America*. London, 1846.

————. *The Collected Works of John Adolphus Etzler*. Delmar, N.Y.: Scholars' Facsimiles & Reprints, 1977.

Evelyn, John. *Sylva, or a Discourse on Forest Trees*. London, 1664.

Everett, Alexander Hill. *New Ideas on Population: With Remarks on the Theories of Malthus and Godwin*. Boston, 1823.

————. *A Discourse on the Progress and Limits of Social Improvement: Including a General Survey of the History of Civilization*. Boston, 1834.

————. *Critical and Miscellaneous Essays*. Boston, 1846.

Everett, Edward. *Orations and Speeches on Various Occasions*. Boston, 1836.

Ewbank, Thomas. *A Descriptive and Historical Account of Hydraulic and Other Machines for Raising Water, Ancient and Modern*. 1842. Reprint. New York, 1850.

————. *The Spoon, with Upwards of One Hundred Illustrations*. New York, 1844.

————. *Life in Brazil: A Journal of a Visit to the Land of the Cocoa and the Palm*. New York, 1856. Making of America.

————. "The Motors: Chief Levers of Civilization." *Report of the Commissioner of Patents for the Year 1849*. Washington City, 1849.

————. *Inorganic Forces Ordained to Supersede Human Slavery*. New York, 1860.

————. *The Position of Our Species in the Path of Its Destiny, or, the Comparative Infancy of Man and of the Earth as His Home*. New York: Charles Scribner, 1860.

————. *The World a Workshop*. 1864.

Ferguson, Adam. *Essay on the History of Civil Society*. 1767. Reprint. New Brunswick, N.J.: Transaction Publishers, 1980.

Feuerbach, Ludwig. *The Essence of Christianity.* 1841. Trans. George Eliot. Reprint. 1854. Marxists.org.

Feynman, Richard Phillips, Robert B. Leighton, and Matthew L. Sands. *The Feynman Lectures on Physics.* Reading, Mass.: Addison-Wesley, 1963.

Fine, Ben. *Marx's Capital.* London: Macmillan, 1984.

———. *The Coal Question: Political Economy and Industrial Change from the Nineteenth Century to the Present Day.* New York: Routledge, 1990.

Finkelstein, Andrea. "Nicholas Barbon and the Quality of Infinity." *History of Political Economy* 32 (Spring 2000): 83–102.

Fogel, Robert William. *Escape from Hunger and Premature Death, 1700–2100.* New York: Cambridge University Press, 2004.

Foster, John Bellamy. *Marx's Ecology: Materialism and Nature.* New York: Monthly Review Press, 2000.

Fourier, Charles. *Le Nouveau Monde industriel et sociétaire, ou Invention du Procédé d'Industrie attrayante et naturelle distribuée en Séries passionnées.* Paris, 1829.

———. *Fourier's Theory of Society.* New York, 1844.

———. *Design for Utopia: Selected Writings of Charles Fourier.* New York: Schocken Books, 1971.

Fourier Society, *The Fourier Society for Publishing the Works of Charles Fourier and Other Eminent Writers on the Science of Industrial Association.* England[?], 1846. Making of the Modern World.

Fried, Albert, and Ronald Sanders, eds. *Socialist Thought: A Documentary History.* Garden City, N.Y.: Anchor Books, 1964.

Friedman, Benjamin M. *The Moral Consequences of Economic Growth.* New York: Vintage Books, 2006.

Fuller, R. Buckminster. *Nine Chains to the Moon.* Philadelphia: J. B. Lippincott, 1938.

Fürstenwärther, Moritz Freiherr von. *Der Deutsche in Nord-Amerika.* Stuttgart, 1818.

Galletti, Johann Georg August. *Allgemeine Weltkunde, oder: Geographisch-statistisch-historische Übersichtsblätter aller Länder.* Leipzig, 1818.

Gellner, Ernest. *Plough, Sword, and Book: The Structure of Human History.* Chicago: University of Chicago Press, 1989.

Georgescu-Roegen, Nicholas. *The Entropy Law and the Economic Process.* Cambridge, Mass.: Harvard University Press, 1971.

Gilje, Paul A., "The Rise of Capitalism in the Early Republic." *Journal of the Early Republic* 16 (Summer 1996).

Gilmore, Paul. "Mechanical Means: Emersonian Aesthetic Transcendence and Antebellum Technology." *Modern Language Quarterly* 65 (June 2004): 245.

Glacken, Clarence. *Traces on the Rhodian Shore: Nature and Culture in Western Thought*. Berkeley: University of California Press, 1967.

Gray, John. *False Dawn: The Delusions of Global Capitalism*. London: Granta, 2002.

———. *Black Mass: Apocalyptic Religion and the Death of Utopia*. New York: Farrar, Straus and Giroux, 2007.

Gray, Simon. *Gray versus Malthus: The Principle of Population and Production Investigated*. London, 1818.

Grund, Francis J. *The Americans, in Their Moral, Social, and Political Relations*. Boston, 1837.

Guarneri, Carl J. "Importing Fourierism to America." *Journal of the History of Ideas* 43 (October–December 1982): 581–94.

Güssefeld, F. L. *Charte von Nordamerica: Nach astronomischen Bestimmungen und den Neuesten Charten von Dalrymple*. Nürnberg, Germany, 1797.

Guyot, Arnold. *The Earth and Man: Lectures in Comparative Physical Geography*. Boston, 1849.

Hansard, Luke James. *Hints and Reflections for Railway Travelers and Others, or A Journey to the Phalanx*. London, 1843.

Harvey, David. *The Condition of Postmodernity: An Enquiry into the Origins of Cultural Change*. Cambridge, Mass.: Blackwell, 1989.

———. *Spaces of Hope*. Berkeley: University of California Press, 2000.

Hatch, Alden. *Buckminster Fuller; at Home in the Universe*. New York: Crown Publishers, 1974.

Hegel, Georg Wilhelm Friedrich. *Encyclopedia of the Philosophical Sciences*. 1817. Available at hegel.marxists.org.

———. *Hegel's Philosophy of Right*. 1820. Ed. T. M. Knox. Reprint. Oxford: Clarendon Press, 1965.

———. *The Philosophy of History*. 1837. Reprint. Kitchener, Ontario: Batoche Books, 2001. Ebrary.

———. *Hegel, the Essential Writings*. Ed. Frederick G. Weiss. New York: Harper & Row, 1974.

Hietala, Thomas R. *Manifest Design: Anxious Aggrandizement in Late Jacksonian America*. Ithaca, N.Y.: Cornell University Press, 1985.

Hodge, Charles. "The School of Hegel." *Princeton Review* (January 1840).

Holmes, George Frederick. "Population and Capital." *DeBow's Review* 21 (September 1856): 217–32.

Homann Erben (Firm). *Kleiner Schul-Atlas Von Achtzehn Homannischen Landkarten*. Nürnberg, Germany: Homann Erben, 1806.

Hopkins, Samuel. *A Treatise on the Millennium: Showing from Scripture Prophecy, That It Is Yet to Come: When It Will Come; in What It Will Consist; and the Events Which Are First to Take Place*. Boston: Isaiah Thomas, 1793.

Humboldt, Alexander von. *Political Essay on the Kingdom of New Spain.* Trans. John Black. London, 1822. Making of the Modern World.

Hume, David, "Of the Populousness of Ancient Nations." *Essays Moral, Political, Literary.* 1777. Ed. Eugene F. Miller. Reprint. Indianapolis: Liberty Fund, 1987.

Israel, Jonathan. *Dutch Primacy in World Trade 1585–1740.* Oxford: Clarendon Press, 1989.

Jevons, William Stanley. *The Coal Question: An Enquiry concerning the Progress of the Nation, and the Probable Exhaustion of Our Coal-Mines.* London: Macmillan, 1866.

———. *The Theory of Political Economy.* London: Macmillan, 1871.

———. *The Principles of Science: A Treatise on Logic and Scientific Method.* New York: Macmillan, 1874.

Johnston, Louis D., and Samuel H. Williamson. "The Annual Real and Nominal GDP for the United States, 1790–Present." Economic History Services. eh.net/hmit/gdp.

Kendrick, Asahel Clark. *Ancient and Modern Civilizations Contrasted.* New York, 1845.

Latour, Bruno. *We Have Never Been Modern.* Trans. Catherine Porter. Cambridge, Mass.: Harvard University Press, 1993.

Lause, Mark A. *Young America: Land, Labor, and the Republican Community.* Urbana: University of Illinois Press, 2005.

Leonhardt, David. "The New Inequality." *New York Times Magazine* (December 10, 2006).

Levi-Faur, David. "Friedrich List and the Political Economy of the Nation-State, *Review of International Political Economy* 4 (Spring 1997): 154–78.

Liebig, Justus. *Organic Chemistry in Its Applications to Agriculture and Physiology.* London, 1840.

———. *Familiar Letters on Chemistry, and Its Relation to Commerce, Physiology and Agriculture.* New York, 1843.

Lindenfeld, David F. *The Practical Imagination: The German Sciences of State in the Nineteenth Century.* Chicago: University of Chicago Press, 1997.

List, Friedrich. *Outlines of American Political Economy, in a Series of Letters Addressed by Frederick List, Esq. Late Professor of Political Economy at the University of Tubingen in Germany, to Charles J. Ingersoll, Esq. Vice President of the Pennsylvania Society for the Promotion of Manufactures and the Mechanic Arts.* Philadelphia, 1827.

———. *Speech, Delivered at the Philadelphia Manufacturers' Dinner.* Philadelphia, 1827.

———. *Das Nationale der politischen Oekonomie.* Stuttgart, 1841.

———. *National System of Political Economy.* Philadelphia, 1856.

Little, John. *The Timber Supply Question, of the Dominion of Canada and of the United States of America*. Montreal, 1876.

Long, George. *America and the West Indies, Geographically Described*. London, 1845.

Lovejoy, Arthur O. *The Great Chain of Being: A Study of the History of an Idea*. 1936. Reprint. New York: Harper Torchbooks, 1960.

Luther, Seth. *An Address Delivered before the Mechanics and Working-Men of the City of Brooklyn*. Brooklyn, N.Y., 1836.

Malthus, Thomas Robert. *An Essay on the Principle of Population and a Summary View of the Principle of Population*. 1798 and 1830. Ed. Antony Flew. Reprint. New York: Penguin, 1985.

———. *An Essay on the Principle of Population and a Summary View of the Principle of Population*. London, 1798. Library of Economics and Liberty.

Man, Thomas. *Picture of a Factory Village*. Providence, R.I., 1833.

Marsh, George Perkins. *Man and Nature; or, Physical Geography as Modified by Human Action*. New York: Scribner, 1864. Library of Congress. American Memory.

Marx, Karl. *Theses on Feuerbach*. 1845. Available at marxists.org.

———. *Capital: A Critique of Political Economy*. Volume One. 1867. Trans. Samuel Moore and Edward Aveling. Ed. Frederick Engels. Reprint. Chicago: Charles H. Kerr, 1906. Library of Economics and Liberty.

———. *Capital: A Critique of Political Economy*. Volume One. 1867. Trans. Ben Fowkes. Reprint. New York: Penguin Books in association with New Left Review, 1990.

———. *Capital*, Volume Three. Trans. Ernest Untermann. Ed. Frederick Engels. Chicago: Charles H. Kerr and Co., 1909. Library of Economics and Liberty.

Marx, Karl, and Friedrich Engels. *The Communist Manifesto*. 1848. Ed. A.J.P. Taylor. Reprint. London: Penguin Books, 1985.

———. *The Marx-Engels Reader*. Ed. Robert C. Tucker. New York: W. W. Norton, 1978.

Masquerier, Lewis. *A Scientific Division and Nomenclature of the Earth*. New York, 1847.

Masur, Louis P. *1831, Year of Eclipse*. New York: Hill and Wang, 2001.

McCoy, Drew R. *The Elusive Republic: Political Economy in Jeffersonian America*. Chapel Hill, N.C.: University of North Carolina Press, 1980.

McKibben, Bill. *Deep Economy: The Wealth of Communities and the Durable Future*. New York: Times Books, 2007.

Megill, Allan. *Karl Marx: The Burden of Reason (Why Marx Rejected Politics and the Market)*. Lanham, Md.: Rowman and Littlefield, 2002.

Menzel, Wolfgang. *The History of Germany, from the Earliest Period to the Present Time*. London, 1848.

Merchant, Carolyn. *The Death of Nature: Women, Ecology, and the Scientific Revolution*. San Francisco: Harper and Row, 1990.

Mill, John Stuart. *Essays on Some Unsettled Questions of Political Economy*. London, 1844. Library of Economics and Liberty.

———. *Principles of Political Economy*. 1848. Ed. Jonathan Riley. Reprint. New York: Oxford University Press, 1994.

Mirowski, Philip. *Against Mechanism: Why Economics Needs Protection from Science*. Totowa, N.J.: Rowman and Littlefield, 1988.

Montesquieu, Charles de Secondat, Baron de. *The Spirit of the Laws*. 1748. Ed. David Wallace Carrithers. Reprint. Berkeley and Los Angeles: University of California Press, 1977.

Morrison, Rodney J. "Henry C. Carey and American Economic Development." *Transactions of the American Philosophical Society* New Ser. 76 (1986): 1–91.

Müller, Johannes von. *The History of the World: From the Earliest Period to the Year of Our Lord 1783, with Particular Reference to the Affairs of Europe and Her Colonies*. Boston, 1840.

Mumford, Lewis. *Technics and Civilization*. New York: Harcourt, Brace, 1934.

———. *The City in History: Its Origins, Its Transformations, and Its Prospects*. New York: Harcourt, Brace, 1961.

Nadeau, Robert. *The Wealth of Nature: How Mainstream Economics Has Failed the Environment*. New York: Columbia University Press, 2003.

Pearson, John. *Notes during a Journey in 1821 in the United States of America: From Philadelphia to the Neighborhood of Lake Erie*. London, 1822.

Perelman, Michael. *The Invention of Capitalism: Classical Political Economy and the Secret History of Primitive Accumulation*. Durham, N.C.: Duke University Press, 2000.

———. *The Perverse Economy: The Impact of Markets on People and the Environment*. New York: Palgrave Macmillan, 2003.

Petyt, William. *Britannia Languens, or a Discourse of Trade*. London, 1680. The Making of the Modern World.

Pickens, Francis Wilkinson. *An Address on the Great Points of Difference between Ancient and Modern Civilization*. Athens, 1843.

Pielou, E. C. *The Energy of Nature*. Chicago: University of Chicago Press, 2001.

Pigou, Arthur Cecil. *The Economics of Welfare*. London: Macmillan, 1920.

Polanyi, Carl, *The Great Transformation: The Political and Economic Origins of Our Time*. 1944. Reprint. Boston: Beacon Press, 2001.

Polk, James K. "Address to Congress." *Journal of the Senate* (June 1, 1841).

Potter, Alonzo. *Political Economy: Its Objects, Uses, and Principles Considered with Reference to the Condition of the American People.* New York: Harper and Brothers, 1840.

Putnam, Oliver. *Tracts on Sundry Topics of Political Economy.* 1834.

Richards, John F. *The Unending Frontier: An Environmental History of the Early Modern World.* Berkeley and Los Angeles: University of California Press, 2001.

Ritter, Carl. *Die Erdkunde im Verhältniss zur Natur und zur Geschichte des Menschen. (The Science of the Earth in Relation to Nature and the History of Mankind).* 19 volumes. 1817–59.

———. *Naturhistorische Reise nach der westindischen Insel Hayti.* Stuttgart: Hallberger, 1836.

———. *Geographical Studies.* Boston, 1863.

Roberts, Jason. *A Sense of the World: How a Blind Man Became History's Greatest Traveler.* New York: HarperCollins, 2006.

Roebling, Johann August. *Diary of My Journey from Muehlhausen in Thuringia via Bremen to the United States of North America in the Year 1831.* Trans. Edward Underwood. Trenton, N.J.: Roebling Press, 1931.

———. Letter to Mr. F. Bähr. Pittsburgh, November 2, 1831. Published as "Pragmatists and Prophets: George Rapp and J. A. Roebling versus J. A. Etzler and Count Leon." Edited by Patrick R. Brostowin and Karl J. R. Arndt. *Western Pennsylvania Historical Magazine* 52 (January 1969).

Roebling, Washington A. *Early History of Saxonburg.* 1924. Reprint. Saxonburg, Pa.: The Saxonburg Historical and Restoration Commission, 1975.

Rossiter, Margaret W. *The Emergence of Agricultural Science: Justus Liebig and the Americans, 1840–1880.* New Haven: Yale University Press, 1975.

Rostow, W. W. *The Stages of Economic Growth: A Non-Communist Manifesto.* New York: Cambridge University Press, 1961.

Rotteck, Carl von. *General History of the World from the Earliest Times Until the Year 1831.* Philadelphia: C. F. Stollmeyer, 1840.

Rousseau, Jean-Jacques. "Discourse on the Origins of Inequality." *Jean-Jacques Rousseau: The Basic Political Writings.* Indianapolis: Hackett Publishing Company, 1987.

Seaman, Ezra C. *Essays on the Progress of Nations: In Productive Industry, Civilization, Population and Wealth.* New York: Scribner, 1846. Making of America.

Shapiro, Isaac, and Robert Greenstein. *The Widening Income Gulf.* Washington, D. C.: Center on Budget and Policy Priorities, 1999.

Sharlin, Allan. "Natural Decrease in Early Modern Cities: A Reconsideration." *Past and Present* 79 (Number 1, 1978): 126–38.

Sheehan, James J. *German History, 1770–1866.* New York: Oxford University Press, 1989.

Simpson, Stephen. *The Working Man's Manual: A New Theory of Political Economy, on the Principle of Production, the Source of Wealth.* Philadelphia, 1831.

Smil, Vaclav. *General Energetics: Energy in the Biosphere and Civilization.* New York: Wiley, 1991.

———. *Energy at the Crossroads: Global Perspectives and Uncertainties.* Cambridge, Mass.: MIT Press, 2003.

Smith, Adam. *An Inquiry into the Nature and Causes of the Wealth of Nations.* 1776. Reprint. London: Methuen and Co., 1904. Library of Economics and Liberty.

———. *The Wealth of Nations.* 1776. Ed. Edwin Cannan. Reprint. New York: Bantam, 2003.

Smith, Crosbie. *The Science of Energy: A Cultural History of Energy Physics in Victorian Britain.* London: Athlone, 1998.

Smith, E. Peshine. *A Manual of Political Economy.* New York, 1853.

Smith, W. Anderson. *"Shepherd" Smith the Universalist: The Story of a Mind, Being a Life of the Rev. James E. Smith.* London, 1892.

Smolnikar, Andreas Bernardus. *Secret Enemies of True Republicanism . . . regarding the Inner Life of Man and the Spirit World.* Springhill, Pa., 1859.

Steinman, David Barnard. *Builders of the Bridge: The Story of John Roebling and His Son.* New York, Harcourt, Brace, 1945.

Stoll, Steven. *Larding the Lean Earth: Soil and Society in Nineteenth-Century America.* New York: Hill and Wang, 2002.

Tainter, Joseph A. *The Collapse of Complex Societies.* New York: Cambridge University Press, 1988.

Thoreau, Henry David. *Anti-Slavery and Reform Papers.* Montreal: Harvest House, 1963.

Trachtenberg, Alan. *Brooklyn Bridge: Fact and Symbol.* Chicago: University of Chicago Press, 1979.

Transon, Abel. *False Association and Its Remedy, or, A Critical Introduction to the Late Charles Fourier's Theory of Attractive Industry.* London: Office of *The London Phalanx*, 1841.

Tucker, George. *The Laws of Wages, Profits, and Rent, Investigated.* Philadelphia: E. L. Carey, 1837.

———. *Progress of the United States in Population and Wealth for Fifty*

Years, as Exhibited by the Decennial Census. New York: Press of Hunt's Merchants' Magazine, 1843.

———. "The Malthusian Theory." *United States Magazine and Democratic Review* 17 (October 1845): 297–310.

Tucker, Richard P. *Insatiable Appetite: The United States and the Ecological Degradation of the Tropical World.* Berkeley: University of California Press, 2000.

Tyndall, John. *Heat Considered as a Mode of Motion: Being a Course of Twelve Lectures Delivered at the Royal Institution of Great Britain in the Season of 1862.* New York: D. Appleton, 1863.

United States. *Index of Patents Issued from the United States Patent Office from 1790 to 1873.* Washington, D.C.: 1874. Making of America.

United States Patent Office. *Annual Report of Commissioner of Patents.*

Walker, Amasa. *The Science of Wealth: A Manual of Political Economy.* Boston, 1866. Making of America.

Wallace, Robert. *A Dissertation on the Numbers of Mankind in Ancient and Modern Times.* Edinburgh, 1753.

Warden, David Bailie. *A Statistical, Political, and Historical Account of the United States of North America; from the Period of Their First Colonization to the Present Day.* Philadelphia, 1819.

Wayland, Francis. *The Elements of Political Economy.* Boston, 1837.

Williams, David. *Lectures on Political Principles.* London, 1789.

Williams, Michael. *Americans and Their Forests: A Historical Geography.* New York: Cambridge University Press, 1989.

Wood, Donald. *Trinidad in Transition: The Years after Slavery.* New York: Oxford University Press, 1986.

Wood, Ellen Meiksins. *The Origin of Capitalism.* New York: Monthly Review Press, 1999.

Woodbury, Levi. *Twenty-Second Anniversary Address before the American Institute.* New York, 1849.

Youmans, Edward Livingston, ed. *The Correlation and Conservation of Forces: A Series of Expositions.* New York: D. Appleton, 1865.

Young, Samuel. *A Discourse Delivered at Schenectady, July 25, A.D. 1826 before the New-York Alpha of the Phi Beta Kappa.* Ballston Spa, 1826.

Acknowledgments

A group of talented students helped me to think through some of the ideas in this book: Erin Lin, Wells O'Byrne, Quyen Vo, Julian Prokopetz, James Schulte, Christian Barjum, David Lyons, and Kalindi Winfield. They wrote and argued like the critical political economists they had become. They made me proud. I gratefully acknowledge the assistance of a descendant of Conrad F. Stollmeyer, Humphrey Stollmeyer of Port of Spain, Trinidad, who shared with me the contents of three letters and offered help with a number of sources. (I am not related to the Stollmeyer family.) Herman Daly and Robert Solow talked with me about economic growth. David Montgomery shared his tremendous knowledge of the nineteenth century by reading portions of the manuscript. I am pleased to acknowledge two great supporters: Lisa Adams, my agent, and Thomas LeBien, editor and publisher of Hill and Wang.

Index

Page numbers in *italics* refer to illustrations.

Etzler, John Adolphus (*cont.*)
54, 58, 64, 76, 82; wife and in-
laws of, 116, 133; writings of,
35, 98, 104, 106; see also *Par-
adise Within the Reach of All
Men, The*
Etzler, Maria Christina Fröbe, 23
Evans, George Henry, 69
Evelyn, John, 167*n2*
Everett, Edward, 19
evolution, 35; social, 18–19
Ewbank, Thomas, 54–55, 70–71
Expansion, Era of, 163–64

factories, 53, 78, *101*, 156; early,
106; textile, 15, 76, 87, 89
fallowing, 155–56
"Farming" (Emerson), 146
Federal Reserve Bank, 85
Ferguson, Adam, 18, 20
Feuerbach, Ludwig, 29, 32, 33, 49
Feynman, Richard, 52
fish, 155
floating island, 9–10, 100–101,
122, 126–27, 136
Forest Reserve Act (1891), 143
4D (Dymaxion) House, 140
Fourier, Charles, 61, 66, 70, 78–
79, 80, 92, 97, 170, 173; Etzler
influenced by, 50, 82; phalanx
communities and, 49–50
France, 59, 74, 92, 105; July
(1830) Revolution in, 35–37
Frankenstein (Shelley), 179*n10*
freedom, 113; economic vs. political, 76–77
French Revolution, 36, 48
friction, 52, 122
Friedman, Benjamin, 160–61, 165
Fruitland community, 48
Fuller, R. Buckminster, 140–42,
178*n2*
futurists, 140

Galbraith, John Kenneth, 153
Gellner, Ernest, 15–16

*General View of the United States of
North America...,A* (Etzler and
Roebling), 35
geodesic domes, 141
geography, human, 110–12
Georgescu-Roegen, Nicholas, 149,
152–53, 181*nn18, 19*
German Ideology, The (Marx), 32–
33
German Settlement Society, 96
Germany, 74, 96, 105; Etzler's
early years in, 22–23; immigra-
tion to U.S. from, 25–27, 34,
35, 37–38, 40, 176*n16*; political
upheaval in, 26, 36–37
God, as agent in human history,
19, 28, 50–51, 61, 80–81, 111;
deterministic view of, 63; En-
lightenment view of, 17–18;
Great Chain of Being and, 144;
see also Providence
Godwin, Parke, 177*n29*
Godwin, William, 63
gold, 62
Gore, Al, 3
Graedel, Thomas, 157–58
gravity, 15, 52
Gray, John, 81
Great Britain, 71, 75, 85, 95; capitalism's beginnings in, 77, 163;
Era of Expansion begun in, 163;
Etzler's emigration society in, *see*
Tropical Emigration Society; rad-
ical working-class politics in, 99;
Satellite demonstrated in, 9, 14–
15, 22; slavery abolished in, 45–
46
Great Chain of Being, 144
Great Depression, 141, 142, 165
Greeley, Horace, 50, 71, 146,
170*n5*, 173*n48*, 177*n29*
Greenspan, Alan, 123
gross domestic product (GDP), 5,
16, 91, 152, 154, 160; in U.S.,
87–88, 162
Guinimita, Bay of, 118

scorched-earth tactics, 172*n31*

Seaman, Ezra, 89–90

Second Seminole War (1835–42), 67

Second Tropical Emigration Society, 125, 133

Shelley, Mary, 179*n10*

slaves/slavery, 35, 45–46, 68, 91, 110

Smith, Adam, 16, 17–18, 60, 81, 83–84, 85, 123, 145, 154

Smith, Erasmus Peshine, 64, 145

Smith, Joseph, 48–49, 177*n29*

Smolnikar, Andrew, 120, 177*n29*

socialism/socialists, 8, 49, 50, 64, 69, 71, 76, 78, 80, 96–97, 99, 104

societies, collapse of, 151–52

solar energy, 45, 53, 54, 56–57, 75, 109–10, 159, 182*n24*

Solow, Robert, 162–63

South, agrarian economy of, 90–91

Southern Quarterly Review, 61

Spain, 119; New Granada colony of, 24

species extinction, 142, 155

Spinoza, Baruch, 17

Spirit of the Laws, The (Montesquieu), 111

stages, economic theory of, 59, 147; *see also* civil society, evolution of

standard of living, 88–89, 140

stationary state, in growth of civilizations, 163

steam engines, 20, 45, 57, 73, 77, 124

Stollmeyer, Charles Fourier, 137

Stollmeyer, Conrad, 96–102, 109–10, 137–38, 175; Etzler's first meeting with, 92–93, 97; as Etzler's partner and promoter, *96,* 97–102; Satellite and, 14, 22, 120–23, 124, 125; as Tropical Emigration Society's trea-

surer, 104, 123–24, 133; in Venezuela, 125–33, 136, 137

Stüler, Friedrich August, 24

sugar, 92, 109–10, 113, 115, 119

Sumner, William Graham, 143

surplus value, 16

suspension bridges, 41, 136, 178*n47*

sustainable development, 153–54

Sylva, or a Discourse on Forest Trees (Evelyn), 167*n2*

Tainter, Joseph A., 151

tariffs, 86

Tariff of 1828, 82

Taylor, Charles, 116, 118, 124, 125

tea, 113–15

technology, agricultural, 35, 71–72; *see also* Satellite

Texas, 92; War of Independence, 67

textile industry, 15, 76, 87, 89

thermodynamics, 54–55, 91–92, 153, 171; first law of, 146, 148; second law of, 55–56, 148–49

Thoreau, Henry David, 48, 102–103

throughput, 16

Timber Culture Act (1873), 143

Tocqueville, Alexis de, 35

Torah, 19

totalitarianism, 165

Trachtenberg, Alan, 136

trade, 61–62, 63, 74, 83, 109

Transcendentalists, 48

Trinidad, 116–17, 126, 131–34, 137

Tropical Emigration Society, 9, 22; constitution of, 105; founding members and officers of, 104, 116; newspaper of, *see Morning Star;* Satellite demonstration and, 119–21; settlement attempted in Venezuela by, 105,